Brevard D. Sinclair

The Crowning Sin of the Age

The Perversion of Marriage

Brevard D. Sinclair

The Crowning Sin of the Age
The Perversion of Marriage

ISBN/EAN: 9783337269678

Printed in Europe, USA, Canada, Australia, Japan

Cover: Foto ©Suzi / pixelio.de

More available books at **www.hansebooks.com**

THE

CROWNING SIN OF THE AGE:

The Perversion of Marriage.

BY

BREVARD D. SINCLAIR,

MEMBER OF THE AMERICAN ACADEMY OF POLITICAL AND SOCIAL
SCIENCE; LATE MEMBER OF THE BAR OF THE SUPREME
COURTS OF OHIO, NORTH CAROLINA, AND OF THE
UNITED STATES OF AMERICA.

Lo! children are an heritage of the Lord. — PSALM cxxvii. 3

Thus saith the Lord, write ye this man childless, a man who shall
not prosper in his days. — JEREMIAH xxii. 30.

Οὐ φονεύσεις τέκνον ἐν φθορᾷ οὐδὲ γεννηθὲν ἀποκτενεῖς. — TEACHING
OF THE TWELVE APOSTLES, Chap. ii. 38.

SCRIPTURAL TRACT REPOSITORY:

H. L. HASTINGS,	MARSHALL BROTHERS,
No. 47 CORNHILL, BOSTON, MASS., U.S.A.	KESWICK HOUSE, PATERNOSTER ROW, LONDON.
Printed in America.	*All Rights Reserved.*

TO

My Wife

THE MOTHER OF MY CHILDREN

TO WHOSE SYMPATHY INSPIRATION AND AFFECTION I AM INDEBTED

IN THUS PREACHING FOR GOD AND HUMANITY

This Book is Inscribed.

PREFACE.

This book was born, not made! No one was more surprised than the author at the profound impression the publication of the following sermon created when abstracts of it appeared in the daily papers of Boston and New York. Although it produced a sensation, it was not in any sense intended to be a "sensational sermon." It was conceived out of a full heart bursting with indignation at a sin so prevalent that one must be conveniently blind not to see it, and a sin of such unblushing audacity, that it is becoming aggressive, and has its propagandists in the church as well as in all ranks of society, who would inoculate others with this moral cancer and satanic gangrene.

If a minister of the Gospel of Christ, in a New England city cannot himself rear a family of children without having the privacy of his correspondence and sanctities of his home invaded by the intrusion of meddlers who would pervert marriage and counsel crime, it is high time that the cry of warning and alarm be raised. And if the Christianity of the nineteenth century cannot endure the rebuke of flagrant crimes, it may be well to go back eighteen hundred years to the days of a purer faith and recall the words quoted on our title-page, from that recently discovered work : *"The Teaching of The Twelve Apostles;"* (A. D. 120-160,)—"Thou shalt not slay a child by abortion, nor what is begotten shalt thou destroy :"—and also to trace the indignant protest of the Church of Christ against the prevailing infanticide of heathendom, as seen in the writings of Justin Martyr, Tertullian, Lactantius, Hyppolytus, and the assemblies of the Church ;—the Council of Ancyra, A. D. 314 having imposed *ten years' penance* upon women who "destroy that which they have conceived, or who are employed in making drugs for abortion."

If certain over-fastidious people insist that the sacred exercises and spiritual meditations of the gospel ministry entirely disqualify the preacher of righteousness for the work of discussing and rebuking the flagrant crimes and iniquities which surround him ; perhaps the ordinary reader may admit that ten years previously spent in the study of the principles of Civil and Criminal Law, and in the prac-

(5)

6   *PREFACE.*

tice of the Legal profession in the highest courts of the State and
Nation, may have availed to supply some of the defects in a merely
theological education, and may furnish one preacher a sufficient
excuse for paying some attention to the diabolism of this world, as
well as to the glories of the world to come.

Preaching as I do from Sabbath to Sabbath in a pulpit standing
directly over the coffined relics of so bold and fearless a prophet
of God as George Whitefield, how could I refuse to lift my voice
against the crowning crime of the land and the age ? With the
evidence of the damning sin before me, and the everlasting Word of
God behind me, forbearance here would be crime and cowardice,
entailing the blood of souls upon my skirts !

One circumstance has encouraged me to be courageous and to
take hope that God's Word will not return unto him void. Letters
have poured in upon me by scores, from every section of New England and from many parts of the United States, urging me to lead
on in this fight for the children and the American home ; and blessing
God that he has led me to cry aloud in this matter, when purity is
throttled by iniquity masquerading as purity itself !

Already have I received word of the good this sermon has accomplished in awakening the conscience, and in bringing light and
peace to disquieted homes   There are "left seven thousand in Israel which have not bowed unto Baal," and I pray God that this
sermon may increase that goodly company, until the crime and vice
will be not only unmentionable but unknown in Christian America.

The author takes this occasion to express his obligation to his
friend and publisher, Mr. H. L. Hastings, Editor of THE CHRISTIAN,
for the matter contained in the closing pages of this book. The
article on "Small Families," emphasizes and illustrates points but
briefly referred to in the body of the work. "Without Natural
Affection" exhibits the Christian philosophy underlying this whole
question, and the extracts from "The Wonderful Law," under the
caption of "Practical Suggestions," make this crusade against
childlessness constructive, and point out that obedience to the
Divine precepts will certainly meet with the Divine blessing.

                                        BREVARD D. SINCLAIR.

Old South Parsonage,
First Presbyterian Church,
Newburyport, Mass.,
May, 1892.

CONTENTS.

I. SERMON.

The Crowning Sin of the Age, pp. 9-25.

II. THE REVIEWERS REVIEWED.

III. THE DECAY OF NEW ENGLAND.

IV. THE VOICE OF THE CHURCH.

V. SMALL FAMILIES.

VI. COMMENDATORY LETTERS.

TEXT.

" Then when Lust hath conceived, it bringeth forth Sin :
and Sin, when it is finished, bringeth forth Death."

James i. 15.

THE CROWNING SIN
OF THE AGE.

THE PERVERSION OF MARRIAGE.

If there were any possible way of arousing the consciences of men and women on vital subjects concerning the will of God, other than the fearless preaching of the truth, I would gladly welcome it.

It is not a pleasant task to tear aside the masks which men wear, and expose the rotten leprosy of sin in all of its pestiferous hideousness.

It was no sinecure, that office of the ancient prophets, to come into Israel from their silent and holy communion with God, and in the elegant court of Ahab or of David, or amid the Pharisaic righteousness of Judah and Israel, to denounce the chosen people for their sins.

However men may differ concerning the ease or difficulties of the prophetic life, surely no one would contend that it was an agreeable office for Nathan to say unto David: "Thou art the man!" It is certainly not one whit more pleasant for the modern prophet to say: "Thou art the woman!" In the nature of the case some sins are more heinous in the sight of God than others, and in many cases these more heinous sins are of so delicate a character that they are never alluded to in the pulpit. Yet the very fact of the delicacy of their environment, renders them more dangerous and insidious.

(9)

The prophetic office has not ceased. The true preacher is still a prophet. Christ himself, the greatest of all prophets, forbore not to lift his voice against every sin which presented itself before him. His servant can, if faithful to his commission, do no less. The minister of the gospel who, faithless to his solemn office and his high responsibilities, allows the people to perish unwarned, is a false prophet, and may well heed that solemn word : "My people are destroyed for lack of knowledge : because thou hast rejected knowledge, I will also reject thee, that thou shalt be no priest to me." Hosea iv. 6; 2 Peter iii.

I should feel myself unworthy of the office I hold as an ambassador of the Lord Jesus Christ, did I not lift my voice in the name of God Almighty against that which I regard as

THE CROWNING SIN OF THE AGE.

It is the paramount sin which lies at the root of our spiritual life. A sin which, secret in its nature, cannot fail to paralyze its pure Christian life, and neutralize every effort for righteousness and holiness which the church puts forth. A sin of such delicacy that people affect to be shocked when it is publicly alluded to, and yet a sin which is practiced, applauded and commended so widely in private, that even the children are not ignorant of its prevalence among their elders. Indeed a sin in which, in many cases, daughters are deliberately nurtured and trained, so that when opportunity is presented for its practice, the conscience is so stultified and suborned by long training and familiarity with its hellish and poisonous consequences, that it is committed without compunction.

People much concerned about the "tithe of mint and cummin" of other minor requirements of nineteenth century Pharisaism, do not scruple to omit the weightier matters of the law of God concerning the sin of which I purpose to speak. There can never be a weightier subject submitted to the enlightened conscience of any Christian community than

THE ETHICS OF MARRIAGE.

The institution of marriage lies at the foundation of the Church and the State. Marriage is the Gibraltar of virtue, the basis of the home, the bulwark of the commonwealth, at once the ward and the guardian of the Church of God. It was founded in Eden by God himself. It was hallowed in Cana of Galilee by the presence and benediction of our divine Lord. It is protected by the laws of all Christian nations, and is in an especial sense fostered, guarded and held sacred by the Christian Church. Upon its sanctity and its integrity, and much more upon the accomplishment through it of the ends of its institution, does everything depend.

The destruction of the end or purpose of an institution is virtually the destruction of the institution itself. I firmly believe that the greatest sin against God, and the greatest crime against society, in this nineteenth century, is the covert attack, which, in one form or other, excused by one consideration or another, is being waged against God's institution of marriage. The Word of God places sin, all sin, just where God finds it, and where all deep search will find it. The root of all sin is to be found not in the accidents of birth, environment, or education, but in lust, concupiscence. Not only so, but "when lust hath conceived, it *bringeth forth sin.*" James i. 15. This is as inevitable as the law that the external fruit is the product of the internal life. "For a good tree bringeth not forth corrupt fruit; neither doth a corrupt tree bring forth good fruit ... For of thorns men do not gather figs, nor of a bramble bush gather they grapes." Luke vi. 43, 44.

Applying this very general principle of the teaching of Christ, as epitomized by the Apostle James, to the subject of marriage, I maintain that any marriage which deliberately sets about the violation of God's law as to the end of its institution, is the product, not of righteousness, or of righteous Nature's laws, but is

THE PRODUCT OF LUST!

Lust pure and simple. The only difference between a marriage of such a character, and prostitution, is that society, rotten to its heart, pulpits afraid to cry aloud against the crime and vice, and the church conformed to the world, have made such a profanation of marriage respectable. To put it in other words, when two people determine to live together as husband and wife, and evade the consequences and responsibilities of marriage, they are simply engaged in prostitution without the infamy which attaches to that vice and crime. Marriage is a divine institution. It was founded by God Almighty. It preceded in creation the institution of the church and civil society. When God created Adam and gave him dominion over the magnificent Paradise of creation, and all created things, He said "It is not *good* that the man should be alone ; I will make him an help meet for him." This was the rationale of marriage. The woman was made for the man's good. Man without woman was incomplete. Humanity without woman was but half created. Adam without a wife was morally unfinished, for God said it was not *good* for the man to be alone. Quaint old Matthew Henry says : " She was not made out of his head to top him, not out of his feet to be trampled upon by him, but out of his side to be equal to him, under his arm to be protected, and near his heart to be beloved."

Whatever modern sinners may dream, there never has been and there never will be any advance upon the morality established by God in Eden. It is my deliberate judgment that the experience of the world, no less than the Word of God, agrees in the testimony that it is impossible for men as a rule to lead clean, pure, virtuous lives, from the cradle to the grave, without marriage.

I would offer as conditions of success to every young man starting out in life, these three fundamental rules of the late Henry Grady of Atlanta: "Never gamble, never drink, and above all marry early." Let a young man be poor, that is a misfortune, not a sin; let a young man be uneducated, that is no crime. But marriage with either of these inconveniences is a thousand-fold preferable to unmarried life with sin, and culture, and millions.

One of the most plausible attacks on marriage comes, from the poisonous advice of people who say that a man should never marry until he has accumulated a fortune, or finds a wealthy bride. In accumulating the fortune, he may, nay he is most likely to accumulate a host of evil and sinful habits, contrary alike to the laws of God and man; and in finding the wealthy bride, he may be securing a woman whose fortune is *with* her, but not *in* her! There are some things in this world, believe me, more valuable than money, and the canons of a spurious "best society."

While the situation of woman is so different from man, by reason of her nature, the self-sufficiency of her life, and the sacred shelter of her home, nevertheless the normal condition of woman is declared by Holy Writ to be marriage. I am aware that the world contains many noble women, who have been blessings not only to the church and the world, but to themselves, who have not shared the heart and home of some son of Adam; yet that is a sinful and unscriptural perversion which would teach woman, that marriage is not also, with some exceptions, the position in life which God intended her to fill. Paul in writing instructions on this subject to Timothy said: "I will therefore that the younger women marry, bear children, guide the house, give none occasion to the adversary to speak reproachfully." 1 Tim. v. 14.

It is not strange that we find the sin of which I speak, commencing its malevolent assault, in the spirit of the times, by attacking the institution of marriage itself. A certain class of older people advise, and a certain class of young people seem to think, that they must begin life where their parents left off. If a young man cannot set up the kind of establishment his father has secured after years of toil and labor, both on his own part and that of his wife, the young man is advised or thinks that he must not marry. This reasoning is vicious, and positively sinful. It is introducing the element of lust,—the lust of money —into the realm where love is queen, and the inevitable consequence is that, " it bringeth forth sin : and sin when it is finished bringeth forth death." How appropriate the words of John in this connection : " For all that is in the world, the lust of the flesh, and the lust of the eyes and the pride of life is not of the Father, but is of the world. And the world passeth away, and the lust thereof, but he that doeth the will of God, abideth forever. 1 John ii. 16.

God never intended marriage contracts to be formed in the same way that a man buys a horse—on the basis of mere money value. This method is such a violation of divine law, that it brings its penalty even in this world, in the unhappiness of thousands of homes, and unfaithfulness to the marriage vows, which is one of the most flagrant sins of our time, witnessed by the adulteries which are so prevalent, and the multifarious records of the divorce courts. No such avalanche of penalty could, in the providence of God, attach to anything, but outrageous God-defying sin !

But none the less terrible in its effects on the morals and religious life of the community, is the diabolic attack on the institution of marriage in the precept and practice of the people, in the utter perversion of its consequences. Children are just as logical and natural a product of marriage as the fruit is of the tree. Marriage is attacked at the root, by the substitution of money or any other lustful consideration, in the place of that mutual love which God gave to man and woman in Eden. But a more

OUTRAGEOUS VIOLATION OF ALL LAW,

natural and revealed, is the cool and villainous contract by which people entering into the marital relation, engage in defiance of the laws of God and the laws of the commonwealth, that they shall be unincumbered with a family of children. "Disguise the matter as you will," says Dr. Pomeroy, "yet the fact remains that the first and specific object of marriage is the rearing of a family." "Be fruitful and multiply and replenish the earth," is God's first word to Adam after his creation. Gen. i. 28. "But we may never hope to have the marriage relation what it ought to be, so long as social usage demands that we pretend it is for any or every object except the real one. Marriage has its secondary compensations, such as the preservation of virtue, companionship, etc."* But a relation entered into which ignores the true end of marriage—the birth and rearing of children, and the peopling of the home, the church and the world,—is in the sight of enlightened manhood a farce and a travesty, and in the eye of God a black and infamous sin. "When lust hath conceived it bringeth forth sin." "Sin is lawlessness," and is so defined by Holy Writ.† Any conscientious physician, who is not an accessory before the fact, or a *particeps criminis*, will testify that the prevention of offspring is a violation of every physiological law of man. Every Christian knows that the offence is a violation of the highest moral law of God.

---

* "The Ethics of Marriage," by H. S. Pomeroy, p.
†1 John iii. 4. Revised Version.

The prevention of offspring is pre-eminently the sin of New England,—it is fast becoming the national sin of America, and if it is not checked, it will sooner or later be an irremediable calamity. This sin, as I have shown, has its roots in a low and perverted idea of marriage, and is fostered by false standards of modesty. In the name of God, and of virtue, how can it be checked unless ministers of God cry out against it? Let us call a spade a spade! Evil has often wrought great ruin in the name of religion. Paraphrasing the dying words of Madame Roland concerning liberty, we may well exclaim, "Oh! purity, what crimes have been committed in thy name!" The cry of purity is now working against purity, in the name of purity itself! I can forbear no longer. I believe that this sin is sapping the foundations of pure religion; and until this Achan of sin is weeded out of the Israel of the church and society, we may expect nothing else but a continued decay of holiness and Christian living. Society is indifferent, the church asleep, and the public conscience is dead in this matter. Men and women do not seem to realize that not only in the sacred Word of God, but also upon the Statute Books of the Criminal Codes of the State, are laws which brand them as criminals and guilty sinners!

The sin is none the less heinous, and the crime none the less wicked when it is performed by those who affect "the best society," or who with unworthy hands take the bread and wine at the communion table of a dying Lord, who pronounced his blessing on the pure in heart. Women, professors of Christ's holy religion, according to evidence in my possession, and evidence which any one may readily obtain, go about advising young married women to forestall the ordinance of God, by preventing or obstructing the legitimate end of marriage, the birth and rearing of children.

Do these same white-walled sepulchres of hell know that they are committing the damning sin of Herod in the slaughter of the innocents, and are accessories before the fact to the crime of murder? Do women in all circles of society, both in the church and out of it, realize, when counselling and practicing these diabolical crimes, from the guilt of which no social standing or church relationship will shield, that they will one day fall under the curse of the Lord, before the great white throne?

This crime is so universal that it is practiced indiscriminately in our midst. I have the evidence in my possession of its being practiced by all classes of society, and I feel that if I do not denounce it in the name of God, that the very stones will cry out! God forbid that I should eulogize the errors or conceal the faults of Romanism, but it is the one church in New England which is a *practical* foe to this hell-born sin, which has fastened its fangs and death-venom in the vital heart of marriage.

Whatever the people of other creeds and churches may profess, the Roman Catholic priesthood, preaches the doctrine that recognizes marriage to be a sacrament, and that what God hath joined together, no man or woman must put asunder with impunity; and I believe that, notwithstanding the errors of the Romish Church, it is to be commended for loyalty to this great law of God, which enforces the truth that the end of marriage must not be profaned, that "children are an heritage of the Lord," and that the innocent, necessary, and God-ordained fruits of marriage are sacred in their lives and persons, born or unborn, however much unnatural and child-hating married people may despise them. Psa. cxxvii. 3–5.

New England is lifting her hands to-day with horror at the thought of Catholic domination. We are told that the Roman Catholics are going to possess New England. Through your sin they may do so. And if you persist in sin, they ought to! In God's providence and in the struggle for existence the fittest survive, and the weakest and wickedest become extinct. And the criterion of the "fittest" of the human race is the standard that those who best subserve the end of God in creating them, shall survive.

When we find the native New Englanders defeating the end of marriage by the prevention of offspring, and the Catholic populations obeying God's laws in rearing families, we are simply seeing the working of God's natural law. It makes no difference to God whether your ancestors

CAME OVER THE SEA IN THE MAYFLOWER,

or in the steerage of a Cunarder; whether your pedigree comes from a Puritan, or an assisted emigrant from Cork; whether you are descended from the proud Huguenots of Navarre, or the Catholic French Canadians; but one thing is of paramount concern to God : He does intend to fill this world with righteousness, and in the progress of divine evolution, He will see to it that the people who violate His laws shall perish from the earth, and that those who obey His precepts shall fill the places of a disobedient people.

It seems to me a travesty on the real condition of things, that the Young People's Society of Christian Endeavor movement, which is the latest religious phenomenon of the century, began in New England. Why there are less young people in New England outside of the Romish communion than in any other part of the country! And if this wickedness continues it will soon come to pass, through your sin, that the places you have filled will be occupied by " the sons of the stranger." If the Romanists will obey God and re-habitate the crumbling, decaying, rotten wrecks of the home, the state, and

the church, by obliterating the sin of preventing offspring, then they will and they ought to inherit and possess the land, so that, as in the days agone, New England
may still boast of a pure home, even if of another religion, over the mantle of which the words of Christ may
be read: "Suffer little children to come unto me, and
forbid them not, for of such is the kingdom of heaven."
So that she may still boast of the integrity of the family,
if not of the state and church which grows out of and is
built alone upon the corner stone of marriage.

God says to New England as he said to the church at
Ephesus: "Remember therefore from whence thou art
fallen, and repent and do the first works; or else I will
come unto thee quickly and will remove thy candlestick
out of his place except thou repent."* God has fourteen
hundred millions of people on this earth, and the extinc-
tion of one population for the reception of another, is
simply God's taking a candlestick out of its place and replacing it with a burning candle.

But the text presents a still higher exhibition of lawlessness, and a still deeper degree of wickedness: "*Sin
when it is finished, bringeth forth death!*" All sin is
progressive. Sin is cumulative and fruitful. One sin
brings on another, until it hatches a vast brood of evils.
The sin of marriage begun in lust, brings forth the sin of
prevention of offspring, and this sin in order to accomplish its purpose "bringeth forth death!" With the
perversion of marriage comes a Pandora's box of wickedness. Death to the innocent, unborn life, death in many
cases to the sinners themselves, who would pervert the
laws of God.

A vast army of women have gone to early graves, and
their death certificates have read "hemorrhage," when

*Rev. ii. 5.

the word ought to have been written " abortion." Now
death to human life, born or unborn, which is not brought
about by the command or act of God, is murder! The
woman who kills herself in attempting to prevent offspring, breaks the sixth commandment twice which says:
"Thou shalt do no murder."* And in the eyes of the
law of the land, and of God, everyone who counsels, as-
sists, procures, encourages, or is in anywise privy to the
crime, is an accessory before the fact! Burn this into
your consciences ye who encourage young women to believe that it is inconvenient and unfashionable to bear
children! Let it startle you in the night watches, as you
are awaked from the sleep of sin, by the voice of offended
nature and an offended God, ye who outrage the commandments of God by innuendoes, and counsel that unborn
children must be killed, even if it kills the mother! In
the name of Him whose minister I am, before the high
court of heaven and the bar of conscience, which is God's
monitor in all pure and honest hearts, I indict all such
people, whether in the silks and draperies of "the best
society," or in humbler homes, whether in the families of
clergymen, or those of their parishioners, as *red-handed
murderers.*

The consequences of this sin may, to a certain extent,
be evaded here on earth. Murder and suicide under the
seal of a lying physician's certificate may perhaps prevent
the infamy and the penalty of human laws, but think you
not that such fearful sinners may escape God, when the
dead small and great shall stand before him. Many a
woman is buried with Christian burial, over whose grave
ought to be placed a tombstone with the inscription:

"HERE LIES A SUICIDE

assisted to the grave by her murderers;—her husband,

*Exodus xx. 13. Revised Version.

her female counselors, and the conscienceless physician."
We might well waste no tears on adults who bring upon
themselves the retributive penalty of death for such outrageous sin, but it becomes a far more sacred question
when we contemplate what this sin against the ethics of
marriage means—when we think of the murder of
children unborn.

I know what the miserable apologists for this vice and
crime say in defense of it. I know the lying anodynes
with which they lull their consciences to sleep. I know
the claim they make that life only begins at birth, or at a
certain time prior to it. But I know that when they
make this claim they lie! I know that the best biological
science of the century says they lie. The claim that
there is more evidence for the existence of a soul at birth,
or at a period prior to birth, than at an earlier period, is
moral jugglery and ethical hair-splitting. I know that an
apple is just as much an apple when the flower which
garlanded it in the spring is fallen, as it is three months
later when unripe it is wrenched unnaturally from the
tree which bore it, or in the autumn when in the process
of nature it falls from the stem and begins its independent
life, alone.

There is no scientist on earth who will undertake to
affirm that when the life of the unborn child has once
begun—and the best science affirms that life has begun
from the first—that there is not life as much as at any
subsequent time before or after birth. Besides this ob-
jective refutation of such miserable defenses of child-
murder, there is subjective proof of the exceeding sinfulness of it, which proves it to be murder. In the Sermon on the Mount our Lord showed most plainly that
sin and crime consists not alone in the bare act, but in the
intent of the heart! To look upon a woman with desire,

or in lust, was to have committed adultery.   To be angry
with a brother without a cause was murder. Matt. v. 21, 28.

What is the *intention*, when the effort is made to prevent offspring?   It is the intention to prevent, and to
destroy human life.   The laws of the land, the conscience
of the most degraded, and the majestic law of God unite
in pronouncing it *murder!*

The women of America weep tears over the deluded
mothers of India and China, who throw their infants to
the crocodiles of the Ganges, or into the "infant towers"
of Canton, and send their contributions to convert them.
They do well.   But will they not confess that they are
equally guilty with their heathen sisters, when they destroy the unborn babes which God has given them in
marriage?   Oh! the offence is rank.   It smells to heaven!
It is commended and practiced so universally that it
has crept into the Church of God, and men and women
who would be astonished to hear that they are not
Christians, and who perhaps with great pretentions pray
for a revival in the church, and for the out-pouring of
God's Holy Spirit, are often the guilty parties.   Women
who denounce drunkenness and other sins of much more
trivial importance, are they not often more infamously
guilty, before God? and "the causers of these time-
less deaths, as blameful as the executioners?"

Let me say then to hypocritical Pharisees, that smoking
a cigar may be a filthy habit, but that abortion is murder!
And not even the mask of self-righteousness, nor the pale
of the church, nor denunciation of the publican, will save
them from the wrath of God, and the anathema : "Depart
from Me ye cursed," "I never knew you!" which
Christ will one day hurl from his judgment seat!

I have only brought the prisoner into court, and ar-
raigned him at the bar of God.   Much more might be said.

I have not uncovered the seething mass of vice and infamy which lies beneath the veiled and studied words of this discourse. There is a deeper hell beneath, only to be portrayed in words which, it seems to me, it is not lawful for man to utter.

I can only stand upon the awful precipice of this horrible chaos of sin and shame, which is interpenetrating society, and cry out for God over the fell miasma of this dismal swamp, full of

"Tangled juniper, beds of weeds,
With many a fen where the serpent feeds."

I would asphyxiate your moral life by leading you further into the dark recesses of this stygian cavern of pollution and crime. And so drawing the curtain of the curse of God Almighty upon the insidious and hell-born sin which in God's name I have denounced, in the brief space left me, I wish to state two or three deductions which our consciences must draw from this discussion of truth in the light of God's Word.

MARRIAGE A SACRED THING.

First and foremost, I exhort you to help the Spirit of God and all true and honest hearts, in making marriage what God intended it to be, a sacred thing, secure against the ravages of the divorce court, the lust of money, the lust of the flesh, and the lust of the eyes. Be it known that there is one and only one way to prevent offspring legitimately,—where Nature and nature's God has ordered it; and that is by a life of celibacy and continence. And let us remember that it is a thousand-fold worse to sin, and to pervert marriage, and to murder, than to raise a family even with the burden of poverty and debt. And oh! may God teach us the spirit of Christ, that we may love the little children, and may it be burned upon the sinful hearts of unmotherly mothers and unfatherly fathers that,

" it were better that a millstone were hanged about their necks and they cast into the sea, than that they should offend against one of these little ones,"—born or unborn! Luke xvii. 2.

Let us learn from this that a marriage entered into with the avowed purpose to prevent offspring, is a meretricious union, in which lust conceives and brings forth sin. Let us also learn that in the execution of this sin, which when it is finished bringeth forth death, that abortion and all the horrid synonyms of the accursed butchery is *red-handed murder!*

Now a word to professing Christians. Almost every winter when the frost strikes us, we procure evangelists, we call meetings, we gather crowds, and we try to "get up a revival." Israel was defeated ingloriously and ignominiously at Ai, when they prayed for God's presence, because the sinning Achan was in the camp, and not until they searched out and *exterminated Achan*, did Israel secure the victory and the presence of God.

A community, a church, or a nation that will submit to the presence of the perversion of marriage, and upholds and practices abortion, may easier expect to turn stones into bread, or stop the flow of Niagara by prayers, and pastors, and evangelists, than to revive and convert sinful hearts and secure the blessing of God.

The perversion of marriage and abortion is the prevailing sin of New England, and is fast becoming the national sin of America! I do not fear but that God will blot it out, as thoroughly as he overturned Sodom and Gomorrah, but I warn New England and America to beware lest God in pulling up this iniquity by the roots will pull them up with it, and replant the waste places with another seed and another stock! For " the time is come that judgment must begin at the house of God: and if it first

begin at us, what shall the end be of them that obey not
the gospel of God? And if the righteous scarcely be
saved, where shall the ungodly and the sinner appear?"
"I am the voice of one crying in the wilderness, pre-
pare ye the way of the Lord, make his paths straight!"
And as John the Baptist to the apostate Israel of old, so
do I preach saying to New England and to every
section of America and the world where my words may
truthfully apply: "Repent, for the kingdom of heaven is
at hand!"

"May the time come again when maternity shall everywhere be recognized as the crown of womanhood, and
when every home in our land shall contain a goodly number of children, as the heritage of the Lord."

Then will our homes be harmonious and happy, and
the church and the state—the product of these homes,—
be prosperous, pure and great; the family, the state and
the church, held together by the bond of mutual protection, shall advance onward and upward: "And a little
child shall lead them!"

THE REVIEWERS REVIEWED.

EUPHEMISM.

The criticisms of the public press both commendatory and adverse, as well as the large number of letters received concerning the sermon on "The Crowning Sin of the Age," have brought to light many phases of the profanation of marriage and the allied subjects. To have considered them all in detail would have diverted me from my main purpose, and so caused my discourse to have missed its mark. One of the patronizing suggestions that has come to me, from several clergymen, is that my sermon should have been "toned down" instead of being clothed with the strong and dogmatic assertions which characterized it. My reply is that of the simple rustic to the demonstrator of anatomy who desired to secure his spinal vertebræ for experimental investigation: "If you take out my back-bone I will throw in the rest!" To eliminate the categorical imperative from the domain of ethics, is to destroy the backbone of "oughtness." And to gloss over the exceeding sinfulness of sin, is all that Satan could ask of a sermon. Euphemism is, I firmly believe, the bane of the modern sermon. Sugar-coated preaching, like a sugar-coated pill is too often inoperative. A sermon against sin, which does not like a quivering spear hit the mark of some guilty soul, is as great a failure as Satan might himself desire. I quote with pleasure in this connection an extract from a letter from L. B. L., a Boston merchant:—

"Too long have our ministers remained silent upon this question. Some of our evangelists it is true, have given 'private talks to men only,' but to such I cannot give my approval, compared to your discourse. The gospel is for the people, the remedy for sin, whether found in Holy Writ or preached from the pulpit, and the *remedy* ought to be preached in such a way, that all may sit under its proclamation and be profited thereby. May God richly bless you, and grant unto you all boldness in the truth."

EXCOMIASTIC.

A recent Scottish writer, noting the criticism of a parishioner upon preachers, says: "Our first minister was a man, but he was not a minister; our second was a minister, but he was not a man."

It is refreshing for a minister, who rejoices in his manhood, to publish the following extracts from a letter which exhibits the *man*, and the pure man in every syllable.

"Roxbury, Mass., Nov. 11, 1891.

"I cannot resist the intrusion of a stranger's congratulatory word. Coming from one outside the church, this commendation may not possess much value, however sincerely offered, but such as it is I give it in the name of Him who always called things by their right names. Your sermon was an inspiration, as much so in kind as were those of Paul's. And the more that men thus inspired and thus guided to speak the truth, for truth's sake, regardless of all other considerations, will do so, the stronger will come the inspiration and the greater consequent good will they do. Your words sound like Scripture, because they are true, and because they do not beat about the bush.

There were two things conspicuous in the preaching of Jesus of Nazareth. He never ridiculed those who differed with or opposed his teachings, and he always spoke the truth, and did not spend his time struggling to disguise it in polite innuendoes The protestant world should be covered so deep with printed copies of that sermon, just as delivered, that it would be impossible for it to see any other printed matter,—not even excepting the Book of books. The latter has lost its force to them until the truth shall have been thoroughly burned in. If you could repeat that sermon fifty-two consecutive times, there might be some hope for at least one New England town to start with, and in time we might be able to call *one* 'The Church of Christ.'

While one preaching of this sermon ought to have its good effect, if you could manage to get the same audience together for 52 consecutive Sundays, you might hope for some good from it. Still for one, I have been so greatly edified by its perusal, and in the knowledge that such a discourse has gone out from a 'Christian pulpit' one time more than I had expected to see, that I would not insist on the other fifty-one times, but will hope that some of the others may get a little courage and take it up where you leave it. Besides there are probably fifty-one other burning topics, upon which you might with great profit set the ball rolling, the proper disposition of which should result in enabling every man and woman in a civilized Christian land to decently provide for the children with which God shall bless them. You are to be *doubly congratulated.* Your avocation in life gives you an opportunity to speak to the people, and you have used that opportunity to speak the truth !   Sincerely yours,   I. N. P."

While I do not sympathize with any general aspersion upon my brethren in the ministry, whom I believe to be more faithful to the cause of truth and of God than any other class of men, yet the above letter is remarkably confirmed by the facts of my own experience. The disparity between the sympathy and commendation which I have received from clergymen and the laity is overwhelmingly on the side of the latter. Ministers are too often afraid to handle the delicate matters referred to, doubtless failing to recognize that "The Word of God is quick and powerful, and sharper than any two-edged sword." The recognition of the temper and force of this weapon will make any David courageous against every Goliath of evil. "Is not my word like a fire saith the Lord, and like a hammer that breaketh the rock in pieces?"

ECONOMICS.

Turning for a moment from the form and method of the attack on the heinous sins which I have denounced, a letter from a prominent Real Estate Agent in Lynn, Mass., opens up another phase of the subject which will startle many, and calls for the righteous indignation of all lovers of the family and the home.

"I have read and re-read with very great pleasure and profit your sermon. I wish you might have touched upon a topic, which we as agents for tenement houses have to meet every day. For instance, a landlord will place in our hands a house to rent, with positive instructions to *rent to no one having children*. A party calls and inquires for a desirable tenement. We are obliged to ask if they have children, and if so, we must answer 'No.'

This to my mind is all wrong, and if you could have met this 'horn of the dilemma' and suggested some remedy, then a party would not reply, 'Must I kill my children in order to secure a tenement?' What is the inducement for a young couple to marry and raise children, if they cannot rent a house to live in as their family commences to increase?

I believe that every one should become the possessor of a home of their own, however humble, and their children *know*, as they grow up, what it is to have and enjoy a *home* in every sense of that endearing word. When many of our landlords—and professing Christian men—having children of their own, utterly refuse to allow their tenements to be occupied by 'families with children,' and when honest and good paying tenants are refused houses, simply because they have one or more dear children, it would seem that some remedy might be devised to remedy this enormous and damnable evil.

And when I have seen the tears fall from the mothers' eyes as they look upon the dear ones God has given them, to know they are refused a roof to shelter them, I cannot think the mother's heart wished that they had never been born!"

Perhaps the skeptical who aver that my sermon is sensational may find much food for reflection here. If a temptation of the most imperative and insidious nature had been devised by brains infernal, to promote the sins of abortion and infanticide among the humbler and plainer classes, who are in all countries the purest and most virtuous, no more successful stratagem could be invented. I am no advocate of those who lift up a voice against capital; but I warn the capitalists of America that "though hand join in hand, the wicked shall not be unpunished!" Men of capital must learn that they are not the owners in fee simple of their tenements, but are merely trustees for God Almighty, the ultimate proprietor. They will one day be called into account for their stewardship. "Woe," says Jeremiah, "to him that buildeth his house by unrighteousness, and his chambers by wrong! Did not thy father eat and drink and do judgment and justice, and then it was well with him? He judged the cause of the poor and needy. But thine eyes and thine heart are not, but for thy covetousness, and for to shed innocent blood, and for oppression and for violence to do it." Jer. xxii. 13, 15–17. There is a remedy for this fell blot on the economics of our Christian Civilization. The remedy is the gospel of Christ, and the awakening of a conscience seared with oppression and covetousness.

SARTOR RESARTUS.

Among the specious arguments advanced apologetically, for the practice of abortion, under its various synonyms, is the plausible plea that the sin is justifiable because of the ill health of the inept mother. But whence the ill health? Do the special pleaders recognize the fact that in the divine arrangement, no dallying with symptoms will suffice, but that the grand assize will turn on causes? Testimony might be produced in these pages from the very highest medical authority, that in the largest number of cases the condition where child-bearing would not be permissible on account of the invalid, has been produced by previous interference with the course of nature in the very sin inveighed against in this book.

Violation of natural law inevitably meets with penalty, and it is but a begging of the question to cause the bar to parenthood, and then plead it in extenuation of the sin primarily committed.

All life is from God. He pours its living tides through human forms, perpetuating families and races, until in the descendants of a single faithful man all the nations of the earth may be blessed. To stay this tide of life, and thwart this divine purpose is a fearful offense against society, against the nation, against God.

Perhaps no one cause is more far-reaching in this direction than the fashions and fashion plates which pervert the minds, distort the bodies, ruin the health, and blast the lives of so many women.

Those parts of the body which God has made flexible, fashion encases in a rigid coat of mail, drying up the fountains of vitality, and cramping and enfeebling the organs of life.

These fashions give us, instead of noble, motherly women, a lot of sickly, nervous, frivolous, hysterical things, whose pallid and cadaverous aspect is suggestive of the sepulchre! Among the fashionable women of the day not one in ten can draw a natural breath to save her life, not one in twenty enjoys the robust health which is her right. Hence, with such a style of dress, healthful and happy maternity is an utter impossibility.

The race that is thus exterminating itself is one of the noblest of earth. God sifted the nations to procure the seed with which to plant our fair America. The root of this evil is practical infidelity, neglect of the Bible, and consequent disregard of God and his laws. It was this which made half the births in Paris illegitimate during the Reign of Terror, and which reaches similar results in European cities where the Bible is not read by the people. It is this same disposition, which, seeking indulgence without regard to obligation, uses the evil resources of modern intelligence to thwart the Creator's purposes. Culture or refinement is not a remedy, but an aggravation. Cultivated and refined Greece and Rome, like Athens, and Corinth, amid the splendor wealth and luxury of the empire, merely produced a population of cultivated and refined brutes, in which vice reigned so wantonly that it produced an emperor who was at once a priest, an atheist and a god! To have a family then was regarded as a misfortune, because the childless were courted with extraordinary assiduity by crowds of fortune hunters.*

"Women," Seneca says "married in order to be divorced, and were divorced in order to marry ; and noble Roman matrons counted the years not by the consuls, but by their discarded or discarding husbands."†

The fashionable, æsthetic and intellectual tendencies of our age, divorced from religion, are rapidly whirling American society into a

---
*Tacitus Germ. 20.   †Sen. De Benef. ill. 16.

similar vortex. The critics have not disdained to denounce my sermon as pessimistic, and do me the honor to call me "the American Tolstoi." If so, then John the Baptist and Isaiah were pessimists, and their burning indignation at the vices of their age far outran the *il penseroso* of the Russian Count.

MARRIAGE AND DIVORCE.

The perversion of marriage and its consequences is an Octopus reaching out its numerous deadly tentacles, and grappling with, and affecting almost every relation of life. It is one of the most fruitful causes of divorce and of the difficulties leading thereto. A prominent manufacturer of Lawrence, Mass., writes as follows:

"Although a stranger to you, I take the liberty to thank you for the stand you have taken in this matter, a stand which requires no ordinary courage in any man. I have felt for a long time that the discussion on the divorce question in New England did not touch the root of the matter, and that other reasons might be given for the freedom from this evil in the Catholic Church, than are made public.

There is no doubt in my mind that when there is marriage without a willingness on the part of the wife to take upon herself the duties of maternity, the closest bond that unites both husband and wife is wanting It is a mere union to gratify their passions, and will result when these passions are satiated in the mutual loathing that leads to divorce. There can be no true mutual respect when such habits prevail. I speak of the wife as the offending party, as I believe that in many cases the husband is more willing to do his part in becoming the father of the family, than the wife. And it is an awful probability that the membership of our churches are grievously sinning in this respect. In no other way can we account for the large number of American families in the church where both husband and wife possess ordinary health, yet have at most but one or two children; in many cases none at all.

And while the base sort of literature on this subject, and means of prevention can be freely obtained, no voice may be raised against this crying evil, without reproach from those who would not have the subject alluded to, lest it shock some prudish ears! May you be strengthened to continue the good work, and meet with the success that you deserve."

While upon this subject, I recur to a letter from a woman in Brooklyn, N. Y., who with true matronly indignation and wisdom, points out the assault which sinning husbands make upon the citadel of their own coveted happiness, in encouraging the sin against marriage by their wives.

The wife who successfully evades the natural consequences of the marriage relation, if tempted to infidelity, soon fancies and perceives how easily she may violate the marital rights of the husband, when the evidence of her complicity in stolen sin is so easily obliterated. Children are said to be the best marriage certificates. They may as truthfully be said to be the greatest barrier against a violation of the Seventh Commandment. The perversion of marriage is a most fruitful cause of adultery, and the sinners who practice it; may profitably study their profanation of the end of the marriage relation in the light of their own fidelity.

A CONGRESSMAN'S VIEW.

"Canton, Mass., Nov. 9, 1891.

Rev. B. D. Sinclair:

I want to thank you for your sermon printed in the Boston Globe this morning. If I had a voice that would drown the thunder of Niagara, I would indorse all that you say in reference to the sin that is crying to heaven.

Another generation has arisen here that "knows not Joseph," and they will soon control Massachusetts and New England in consequence of that which you denounce. It is high time that the pulpit, the press, and the platform should cry out.

The "Committee of One Hundred" who hold meetings in Boston, denounce the opponents of the public schools, and go home to one solitary child or none; and the opponents of the public schools go home to half a dozen or more.

The free public school, the Christian Sabbath, all the other institutions that we hold dear, and the perpetuity of the Republic itself, are in danger, from the destruction of the American people, by the causes pointed out by you. Once more I thank you for your bold and fearless utterances upon this subject. I trust the same may have a wide circulation.   Very Respectfully,

ELIJAH A. MORSE.

A note to Hon. E. A. Morse, M. C. asking for the liberty of publishing his patriotic and encouraging words brought forth the following additional letter:

"Rev. B. D. Sinclair:

I have the honor to acknowledge receipt of yours of the 12th. You are at liberty to make any use of my letter that you see fit. If I had known that it was to be published, I would have made it stronger and said more.

You deserve the lasting gratitude of all lovers of their kind. There is a trial going on in Brockton now, of a woman who keeps a house where the crime you describe is perpetrated. Among the witnesses who testified and were summoned by the government, is the wife of a prominent physician in this district, who made no secret of saying that she had resorted to this woman's treatment, that the treatment was successful.

This crime against God and man is not confined to the poor. It is largely common among the rich and well-to-do. Like Isaiah of old may you have grace to "cry aloud and spare not" and lift up your voice like a trumpet, and "show my people their sins, and the house of Jacob their transgression."

Yours for God and home and native land, and the perpetuity of the ancient New England family of Puritan and Protestant lineage.

ELIJAH A. MORSE.

"HANDS UP!"

This is a familiar utterance of western banditti. Hands are often lifted up by assailants also. Already my friends the critics, have raised the alarm of "indelicacy" over my sermon, and have "lifted up their hands in holy horror," because a minister should so outrage the proprieties of Sodom and Gomorrah, as to call attention to the secret sins, which are being practiced in fancied immunity, when more trivial vices are reproved to withdraw attention from the grosser crime.

The following letter from a gentleman in Springvale, Maine, is a genuine tonic amid the depressing influences of prudishness and mock modesty.

"I am so impressed with the absolute truth of your sermon that I cannot resist the temptation to offer my congratulations to one who so fearlessly handled the question of the perversion of the ends of marriage. It is the crying sin of New England, and unless the church be aroused in the matter, the day of doom for New England society is near at hand. No doubt many hands will go up in holy horror to think that so delicate a matter should be preached upon from the pulpit, and possibly some of your own church members will 'wish that Mr. Sinclair had not talked so.' But you may put all such persons down as guilty of the sin condemned! Please accept my sincerest thanks, with the earnest hope that the sermon may, to a great degree have the effect of arousing the women of New England to a sense of whither they are drifting."

GUILTY HUSBANDS.

It was not by any means my purpose in the sermon to divert the arrows of denunciation from reaching any who are guilty of a violation of marriage ethics.

"Oh! many a shaft at random sent,
Finds marks the archer little meant."

In saying "Thou art the woman!" I have also laid the indictment for the father, "Thou art the man!"

The following from an earnest woman of Newburyport, Mass., with a message brimful of truth, demands a place here in justice to a good cause.

Among the criticisms and comments that the recent sermon on marriage called out, I cannot help wondering if it occurred to anybody else as it has to me—to go a step further into the wilderness than the preacher did—and while acknowledging the full force and truth of all that he said, and more, ask *why* are all these things so? Who is to blame for it? And these points being answered according to various individual lights and experiences the next, and to me inevitable question, follows: " *What* are you going to do about it? "

It is generally now as it was in the days of Adam—whenever the voice of the Lord reaches man with any accusing force his answer is still the same:—" The woman that thou gavest me, *she* tempted me." And in this special and particular case, nine men out of ten would protest vigorously that "*they* were not to blame; the customs and claims of society; the dread of physical suffering; the inconvenience or expense; or restraint imposed by the cares of a young family; "—all these or similar reasons conspire to influence women against the " natural and logical result of marriage."

Myself, "but yet a woman," I am convinced that we have always borne more a thousand times than our share of the reproaches and contumely resulting from men's indulgences, ever since that unfortunate scene in the garden of Eden; and that, from that time down to the present and from that event, so incessantly and unjustly brought up against " the woman"—to the subject which Mr. Sinclair has so powerfully handled, there is no fault, misfortune or sin that a woman can be guilty of, that some "he" or other is not more truly responsible for than she is.

Not that " two wrongs make a right," as the saying is, or that the evil or corrupt influence of any man *ought* to be any excuse for the wrong doing of any woman. But we are considering things as they *are*—not as they ought to be. So put the blame where it belongs. Cast the beam out of thine own eye, and attack the men, rather than the women, even by insinuation or implication.

Why do we this, or any other evil, or vanity, or foolishness? Why do we sacrifice ourselves, our comfort, our health,—the domestic ties that all women in their real hearts love and seek? For the same reason that we indulge those vanities; the same reason that we control our tempers,—that we assume a smile rather than a scowl or a sigh, or even wear "blue" when our hearts feel black;— to please, gratify or pacify some man or other, who after all is more likely than not to treat us as the swine did the pearls.

Few, if any women object of or for themselves to the confinement of family cares. It is only for the sake of the men whose property they happen to be, that they try or wish to avoid the duty, self-denial, anxiety or even suffering necessary for bringing up a family of children. And if the men would fulfill even the smallest fraction of the duties which belong as much to one parent as to the other, the women would willingly, if not gladly, endure the pains as well as the pleasures which result from marriage, and fill up the good old New England families which are, "Oh, the pity of it—!" growing so lamentably and lonesomely small and thin.

Yes, Mr. Sinclair, your " eyes have seen the fearful sign to which our eyes are blind." It has been yours to openly and forcibly call our attention to it, and to try arouse us to a horror of it.

Now in the name of all women who love our homes, who would love our children (if we had any), go on. Do not stop here. Denounce *the men* who deprive us of our birthright of domestic happiness. Call them to account for the indulgences which so weaken us that we are often physically unable to achieve that for which we are willing to suffer. Call them to account for the selfishness which makes it often impossible for women to indulge themselves in the comforts necessary to the conditions of successful child-bearing and rearing. Call them to exercise the tenderness, the consideration, the patience towards their wives in that condition which they would show to any animal in their possession, instead of laughing at us, or making us the subject of ribald jokes; teach them to feel for us something more than the little-better-than-his-dog, a-little-dearer-than-his-horse, feeling; show him that his duty and responsibility does not begin and end with providing merely food, shelter and such clothing as may be for his child as well as his wife,—and we women will give you no cause to call us murderers, abortionists, or suicides. Teach the men, instead of the women, that they should make themselves companionable, agreeable after marriage as well as before ; to study a little the self-denial and self-sacrifice which we have studied so long. So shall a race spring up and call you blessed: who shall honor their father and their mother because they see them honor each other; and love each other because their parents loved them before they came into the world, as well as afterward. Truly it was said that a child's education begun nine months before it was born; and if it be along the lines of loving consideration and gratitude there will be fewer cases of reprehensible or unfilial conduct in the next generation than there have been in this one.

Why is it that so many children who are known as nice " pretty behaved," promising boys, grow up to be such wretches as they too often prove ? Because there comes a time when they follow their father's example rather than their mother's precepts , when too often their own fathers lead and encourage them to be what they call "manly," "self-reliant," and so on, against all the prayers and beseechments which their poor, helpless, lonely mothers can put forth. Then the dear good boy becomes—thanks to the " man " whose child he is—a "chip of the old block,"—and the mother looks on in agony which exceeds that which brought him into the world, to see the child she loved and suffered for, stolen from her, and made into a creature for some other poor woman to be deluded by for a time—and after a while to learn in her own turn—to either dread or despise; or if the child be another woman, to see her suffer the griefs, sorrow and misery in her turn. What wonder that so many women dread, and, if possible, avoid child-bearing?

The sermon was able, was eloquent—was in fact everything that it ought to be, so far as it went. Now preach some more, Mr. Sinclair, but do not preach to old maids, or to young boys and girls who go to listen from vulgar and prurient curiosity. Preach strictly to married men or those about to be married, and married women."

"THAT OLD SERPENT, THE DEVIL."

"Murder will out," is a proverb that has passed indelibly into current speech. One who has made a study of this subject cannot fail to recognize the slimy trail of the serpent, on this question, as as he leaves his impress upon the minds and hearts of people, otherwise good. Many entertain an honest enquiry in this vital matter of "having" children. Let the following extract from a letter from a resident of Boston serve as a sample of the universal query. I shall endeavor to answer the question frankly:—

"I have one child two years old after three years of marriage, *and when we feel the time has come*, if the good Lord is willing, more may come, but I maintain that, until we see our way clear to take care of another helpless love, until then we are justified in not having it. Of course, I may be wrong; and if so why I hope for light. I write this to ask if I am, in your opinion, very far from right?"

As far from right as the east is from the west! This letter commends itself for the manly frankness of the writer, who is apparently an honest searcher after truth, and only voices that which the ear does not often hear, but what has entered into a large proportion of the human heart.

The question is not one of expediency, but a question of absolute right and wrong. Is it right or wrong to violate the laws of nature and of God? Let the conscience give her only answer! A distinguished physician has well said: "It is surprising to what an extent the laity believe that medical science knows how to control the birth-rate. Just here let me say that I know of but one prescription which is both safe and sure, namely, *that the sexes shall remain apart.*"*

The question of support herein involved, however difficult from a social standpoint, is easily made plain from the standpoint of morality

* H. S. Pomeroy, M. D. "Ethics of Marriage."

and religion. God never created a mouth without food to fill it.*
And he created covering for every body which he has made. Probably He will not provide silks and satins and Spanish laces for every
child, but when was this affirmed to be either necessary or essential
to the rearing of children ?

Human pride, and not God, or inconvenient conditions and circumstances, will thus be seen to be at the root of this question. Judged
by the ability of a day's human labor to purchase staple human
food and clothing, this decade has seen the easiest conditions
of human life within the range of authentic history, and the world
contains to-day, more and better food and clothing, and other
creature comforts per capita of the human family, than ever before.
In other words, *food and clothes have multiplied more rapidly than
mouths.*†

Another typical case appears in a letter which is of too confiden-
tial a character to make copious extracts. I quote: "I am engaged
to marry . . . I want to know the truth. I am a young man, and
am earning $2.25 per day. Now in your sermon you claimed that
it was every man's duty to marry young, and to raise a family of
children. But the one thing that impressed me most and fairly
horrified me too, and made me feel that the great pleasure of a nice
home, adorned with a sweet loving wife which I had looked forward
to with so much pleasure was going to fade away.

Why? Because you claimed that the only legitimate way to
prevent offspring was by living a single life. I perfectly agree
with you in cases of abortion. But you have just torn my happy
plans all in pieces. I had what I considered very high ideas in
regard to married life, but one of which, if carried out is a sin against
God from the standpoint you have taken. We had planned so
many times to go three or four years without children, and during
that time *enjoy married life*, and meanwhile save what we could.
Now, plainly, *we should like to have about two children* . . . I want
to hear from you again, for I want to know the truth."

The truth is, and the truth must be told, for ignorance is plainly
the trouble here, coupled with the lust of money, that there is no
chapter nor verse in God's revealed law, nor in the laws of nature,
which specifies the number of children any couple shall or shall not
have. And the further advice must be frankly given to this young
man, who appears to have a conscience, and a tender heart, to do his
duty manfully, and leave the rest with God. Duty here contains
the principles not only of marital fidelity and responsibility, but

* Luke xii. 24, 27, 28.
† "Is Man Too Prolific?" H. S. Pomeroy, M. D.

also *temperance.* Intemperance in any of the legitimate passions is lust. Desire for riches and luxuries as a higher aim than paternity or maternity is lust. " When lust hath conceived, it bringeth forth sin, and sin, when it is finished, bringeth forth death."

It does not seem to be generally known that in order that the human race go on reproducing itself, certain conditions are indispensable. If every woman married, and every woman had four children, population would remain just stationary.

If every marriageable adult man and woman, in a given community were to marry, and if every marriage proved fertile, on the average, to the extent of four children, then under favorable circumstances, that community would just keep up its numbers, neither increasing nor decreasing from generation to generation.

If less than all the adult men and women married, or if the marriages proved fertile, on the average, to a less degree than four children apiece, then that community would decrease constantly.

In order that the community may keep up to its normal level, therefore, either all adults must marry and produce to this extent, or else fewer marrying, these few must have families exceeding on the average. four children, in exact proportion to the rate of abstention.

If every man and every woman in a given community were to marry ; and they were in each case to produce two children, a boy and a girl ; and assuming that these children were in every case to attain maturity, then the next generation would exactly reproduce the last, each father being represented by his son, and each mother by her daughter. But as a matter of fact, all the children do not attain maturity. On the contrary nearly half of them, by the statistics, die before reaching the age of manhood and womanhood, in some conditions and countries more than a half.

Roughly speaking then, it may be said that in order that two children may attain maturity, and be capable of marriage, *even under the most favorable circumstances*, four must be born.

The other two must be provided to cover risks of infant, or adolescent mortality, and to insure against infertility or incapacity for marriage in later life. So that even if every possible person married, and if every married pair had four children, we should only just keep up the number of our population from one generation to another.

It is not necessary to say that not every possible person does marry. Therefore it is clear that each actual marriage is, on an average, fertile to considerably more than the extent of four children.

Mr. Grant Allen has made this clear, in some "Plain Words on the Woman Question," in the *Fortnightly Review*. These facts are recognized as axioms by all students of political and social science.

Applying them to New England and America, it will thus be seen that if the native born American mothers shirk their natural duties, they in so far impose a heavier task upon the Catholic and foreign population.

Mr. Grant Allen has demonstrated that an average production of six children to a family, is the very fewest number that the British Isles can do with.

Dr. Pomeroy has also claimed with reference to America, that in order to preserve our present population, four births to each couple are necessary, and that five would only allow for a moderate increase,

"HOLD THE FORT!" FROM CLERGYMEN.

Minneapolis, Minn., Nov. 16th, 1891.

" My Dear Brother :

Allow me to express my hearty appreciation of the sermon recently preached by you on the ethics of marriage. Many voices will doubtless be raised in censure against you, but I desire to be among those who will say ' God bless you,' for your noble courage. You wielded a sharp, but polished shaft. May God direct its glittering point home to every guilty heart! I hope your good people and all the other home-loving people of the land will hold up your hands while you wage this warfare against a crime which is so prevalent and so infernal. My endorsement of your sentiments may give you no pleasure, but it does me good to express my thanks to you for the good service you have rendered the cause of Church and State. Most sincerely yours,

WILLIS A. HADLEY."

Pastor Lyndale Congregational Church, Minneapolis, Minn.

Charlestown, Mass., Nov. 10th, 1891.

" My Dear Brother :

I have just finished reading your sermon. I want in a brotherly way to commend your brave utterance and thank you in behalf of humanity. I know we do not need praise for doing our duty, but I also know that sympathy is comforting, especially when the hornets are thick as they soon will be about your head, unless you have a remarkably pious congregation. May the Lord bless you for it, and may your bow abide in strength for many years to come.

Fraternally,

G. M. SMILEY."

Pastor Monument Square M. E. Church, Charlestown, Mass.

New Bedford, Mass., Nov. 18th, 1891.

"Dear Brother:

I congratulate you upon your courage and ability to deal with the greatest modern social evil. I recently treated the same subject in a part of a discourse which I preached to my people. I was not able then, nor am I at any time, to present it with the pointedness and boldness which you have done in the discourse before me. I wish that you might have it printed in cheap tract form, so that it might have a wider circulation than it could have without it. I think the sin is more general everywhere, even besides New England, than one really knows. The Lord bless you in your crusade against the polite crimes of the 'best' society. Yours very fraternally,

JAMES MITCHELL."

Pastor First Presbyterian Church, New Bedford, Mass.

Newton Highlands, Mass., Nov. 10th, 1891.

"Dear Brother and Comrade:

Will you allow me to extend to you the right hand of hearty fellowship and sympathetic approval regarding your sermon. I thanked God when for the third time I re-read your fearless utterances of the living truth. It made my heart rejoice, for the sound of your trumpet was not uncertain ; and the target at which you aimed was not hidden behind a fog of meaningless verbiage. But thick and fast, and incisive as the strokes of a battle-axe, your words of stern uncompromising denunciation fell full upon the front of the hideous leprosy that walks and lives and has a place even in the highest circles of American, and especially New England social life. I thank you my brother, my comrade, for the inspiration of your courageous example. I know something of what it means to stand before a cultured, refined and conservative audience and proclaim the bold, uncompromising and unflinching truths of God. I know something of the thrill that runs along one's veins when striking at a morality-insulated conscience, the burning, branding words of the living God. It is like the whiz of bullets and the clashing of sabres on the battle field. The naked truth is like a naked sword-blade for execution. But alas how many pulpits are but empty ornamental scabbards of parade day. God bless your words and cheer you in the conflict! Yours truly,

FRANK BARTON."

Pastor M. E. Church, Newton Highlands, Mass.

Boston Highlands, Nov. 18th, 1891.

"I want to thank you, while I offer devout thanksgiving to God for your able, timely, and as I believe divinely inspired sermon on the marriage state. May God touch your lips as he did the prophets of old. We sadly need more of such faithful preaching from the heart. Yours for victory through Christ,

E. D. MALLORY."

Pastor Grove Hall Union Church, Boston Highlands, Mass.

These cheering letters coming spontaneously from brethren in the

ministry, most of them utter strangers to me, only fortify me in
believing that the time is ripe for leading a crusade against the most
insidious vice, the Crowning Sin of the Age. Doubtless many of the
faithful clergy of America are only waiting to say " Amen ! " And
I shall believe that the foregoing are but samples of the heaving
conscience of the faithful preachers of the Word throughout
America. If the clergy are the best authorities on the theological
side of this question, the medical profession are the experts on the
physiological side. I turn now to the

TESTIMONY OF PHYSICIANS.

And first I quote from the much valued letter of a distinguished
physician of Boston who has made a life study of " The Ethics of
Marriage, '* and has written the classical work on that subject, besides another very readable and convincing pamphlet on the ques-
ion : " Is Man too Prolific ? "

Boston, Nov. 9th, 1891.
" My Dear Sir and Brother :
I have read with great interest a digest of your sermon. I am
called a crank on the subject. For years I have been studying and
writing upon it. Incidently I have suffered and am suffering bitter
persecution, because of my position. It is a comfort to me to know
that there is at least one New England Protestant pastor who has
right convictions on this subject, *and has the courage of his convictions. Macte Virtute! Amicus Meus!*
Your sermon will probably bring you a good deal of persecution,
but do not be afraid ! 'One with God is a majority!' and God is
surely on our side. Sincerely yours,

H. STERLING POMEROY, M. D."
With Paul I can say "afflictions abide," in consequence of my
sermon, " but none of these things move me ! " A prophet of God
who expects popularity is on the road to Tarshish, but not Nineveh !
The following letter is from Henry Root, M. D., Surgeon 54th
and 58th N. Y. Vols. ; Bvt. Lieut. Col. U. S. Vols.; Vice President,
Society of the Army of the Potomac.

Whitehall, N. Y., Nov. 13th, 1891.
" Reverend Sir :
Please permit me to thank you for the reading of the sermon to
yours in the New York Press, Nov. 10, on a heinous sin that is not confined to New England. As a physician I can testify to the enormity
of the evil. The insult of being asked to assist in preventing the
further growth of an infant in committing murder, has to be ignored :
but the crime can be averted many times by ignoring the insult and

* Funk & Wagnalls Publishing Co., N. Y.

giving Christian advice. As you speak of Romanists as better than Protestants in the matter, I would say that I do not find it so in my practice. I could write much to sustain your position, but I hope you will not need it from me or others remote from your own city. I write in haste lest days go by and the word in season be lost. I should be glad to hear more of your good work.

Very respectfully yours,

HENRY ROOT, M. D."

As to the comparison of the relative guilt of Protestant and Catholic in this matter, it becomes me to say that it is not my province here, to investigate the reasons why the Catholic families have a larger number of children relatively than Protestant. It is the wide-reaching consequences of the undeniable fact to which I have endeavored to attract serious attention. As to the malpractice of Catholics, I call Dr. Root's attention to the words of Professor Thomas Addis Emmet, M. D., LL.D., ex-president of the American Gynecological Society, etc., etc., in a prefatory note to the "Ethics of Marriage," where he points out that this sin is never committed by Catholics who live in accordance with their belief and teachings.

"I have been in practice" says Dr. Emmet, "over thirty-six years, and for twenty-six years it has been devoted entirely to the treatment of the diseases peculiar to women. As a result of this experience I can in all truth state the fact, that these sins are not committed by the Jews or Catholics. I cannot recall a single instance of either practice, when the individual lived up to her belief: so long as she was what the Catholics term 'practical,' in practice they were pure. Every Jew and every Catholic is taught the duties of married life. Each child born is accepted as an additional evidence of God's especial favor. The Catholic is taught to regard marriage as one of the sacraments, and the slightest deviation from all pertaining to such a belief is a mortal sin."

The Catholic doctrine is, that children must be reared according to nature's promptings, and that it is wicked under all circumstances to prevent the advent into the world of souls intended to be brought by God through marriage; and doubtless this is the Protestant doctrine too, so far as any doctrine is taught by ministers and Christian physicians; as it is also the doctrine of the nation, which by state and United States' laws prohibits these crimes under the severest penalties, and excludes from the mails advertisements and appliances designed to facilitate their commission. The trouble is not with the *doctrines* of any sect, but with the *practice* of persons who are thoughtless, uninformed, and wrongly instructed in private; while in public unfortunately the subject is neglected, and the sin too often ignored.

In a brief work recently published, "The Supreme Passions of Man," Dr. Paul Paquin, late Professor of Comparative Medicine in the Missouri State University gives the results of a series of investigations made by him on this subject, which maintains, upon extended investigation, the assumptions which I have made the basis of comparison between Catholics and Protestants in the matter of the birth rate. He says:

"Of 500 women in six different denominations, married not less than five, nor more than fifteen years, selected indifferently among the well-to-do, taking care not to include anyone who had lost a single child even, the following was obtained. Of 100 in denomination A, (Protestant,) 18 are childless; of 100 in denomination B, (Protestant,) 16 are childless; of 100 in denomination C, (Protestant,) 9 are childless; of 100 in denomination D, (Jew) 8 are childless; of 100 in denomination E, (Roman Catholic,) 3 are childless; of 100 in denomination F, (Greek Church in Europe,) 2 are childless." These investigations were made through church channels, records, family history, etc."

In a letter to the author, J. Farrar, M. D., of 28 King St., Boston, writes:

"Let me say as a physician of over thirty years' experience, the worst half has never been told by you or any other man. It is a pity, too, that the people are not ready and anxious to hear the truth. Still those guilty of what the late Rev. Dr. John Todd of this state, called 'Fashionable Murder,' expect to enter the gates of Heaven, without repentance. * * * I can give you evidence to cover every point on which you have thus far spoken."

HEREDITY.

The exact science of our times has, after a prolonged and tortuous search, arrived at the conclusion of the divine law given to Moses: "*I the Lord thy God am a jealous God, visiting the iniquity of the fathers upon the children.*"

The axiomatic verity of this dogmatic statement is unquestioned when applied to disease and the predisposition to physical weakness of any kind.

None the less real, is the application of the same law to the mental and moral inheritance of children. Those who have diligently observed and studied this question assert with a confidence which is appalling, that if the promise is to parents and to their children, in the divine gift of moral and mental well-being, it is equally true that the curse of God Almighty for violation of physical and moral law, is perpetuated to the third and fourth generation.

If we find that a loving and obedient regard on the part of parents for physical, mental and moral law, inevitably results in a progeny possessing physical beauty, proportionately good mental capacity, and high moral possibilities, what may we not expect to see in children, when the reverse is deliberately invited by sinning parents?

What must the next generation be, if they are the descendants of parents who speak of them as " accidents," whose mothers looked forward to their birth with sorrow, and who regarded that sequence of natural and divine law which brought them into being, as an inconvenience, an imposition?

What must be the physical characteristics of a generation of children whose unnatural mothers regarded them as " things," rather than human beings, before birth? And who can wonder at filial impiety, crime, and murder, in a child whose very soul has been steeped in hatred and murder by the mother, who, previous to his birth has in every way hated and endeavored to circumvent his existence? As surely as like begets like, as absolutely certain as the law of pre-natal heredity, is it an undeniable fact, acknowledged by the medical profession, and apparent to all observers, that a child conceived in such iniquity and brought forth in such cruel sin, will fall below the high standard of mental and moral qualities, even if in the paradox of nature it may be so fortunate as to develop a symmetrical and robust physique. The imbecile asylums of America contain many unfortunates who might well serve as models for the chisel of the sculptor, or the brush of the painter, yet whose mental and moral natures are but the unerring fruition of parental effort to prevent their being ; and of that state of mind which, instead of regarding offspring with love and solicitude, is filled with vexation, confusion and mortification, in view of the false tenets of a polluted social " set, " which regards child-birth as "bad form !"

And shall we not also, in this way explain much of the deformity, the monstrosity, which in the physical, as in the mental offspring, is otherwise unaccountable?

Not once or twice, but many times have conversations been heard in drawing rooms in this civilized and Christian land, when a woman who is a wife in the eye of the law, and a mother by God's ordinance, has introduced her young child to another woman with the remark, aside, "This is my little disappointment." The righteous Nemesis of an offended God and offended nature loses no opportunity to make the appellation as thorough and as real as its utmost import. A child that in its very inception and birth is a disappointment, is in every way likely to be a disappointment. And may not a minister of Jesus Christ add that in the day of Judgment the disappointment of such a parent will shrivel into a keener mortification before the sentence of eternal condemnation: "Inasmuch as ye did so to one of these my little brothers, ye did so to me?"*

Many a man and woman can echo a sentence from a letter received by me from Portland, Oregon: "Let your good work go on. Thousands of lives will be saved, and thousands of persons will live to unconsciously thank you for their existence. I am thankful that my mother was not one of those 'red-handed murderers,' of whom you have spoken. Though spared myself, how could I forgive her, if I felt and knew that she had destroyed my brothers and sisters."

And what must be the diabolical state of mind of those victims of this unnatural sin, who although spared by the overruling providence of God from the efforts of unnatural parents to destroy them before birth, are yet born into the world the heirs of sin, and malice and murder!

Unless the consciences of parents are aroused and quickened, the speedy ruin and ultimate extermination not only of whole families but *whole races* is the inevitable consequence. Perhaps it is best it should be so! Perhaps after all, this is God's method of sifting the world of these latter day examples of pre-Noachic wickedness and crime, in order to re-people the world with a purer race, who bearing more and more upon their hearts the image of Him, who "like as a father pitieth his children," so pities them that fear him ; are devoted in heart and soul to the interests of the best "heritage of the Lord," the children. For "even so it is not the will of your Father which is in heaven, that one of these little ones should perish." Matt. xviii. 14.

VIRTUE ITS OWN REWARD.

One of the sophistries of the age, far more prevalent than the casual observer may surmise, is the wide-spread impression that large families deteriorate the average ability of each individual member. It is boldly argued by some that to produce the most stalwart and perfect children, physically and mentally, the number

*Matt xxv. 40. Syriac Version.

in each family must be artificially restricted. There are people who think one, or, at most, two children very well, but they make every effort to see there shall be no more. But a family which is too small is a vastly greater calamity than one that is too large. Often an only child gives more trouble than the whole of a large family; and it certainly never as much joy. Dr. Smiles tells us that a lady, who with her husband, had inspected most of the lunatic asylums of England and the Continent, found the most numerous class among the patients was almost always those who had been " the only child," and whose will had therefore rarely been thwarted or disciplined in early life.

A very superficial examination of the families from which the great historic names, the conquerors, the poets, the statesmen, the geniuses of the world have sprung, will show that they have been large, often very large families. Out of divine love, "God gave to Heman fourteen sons and three daughters. All these were under the hands of their father for song in the house of the Lord, with cymbals, psalteries, and harps for the service of the house of God." 1 Chron. xxv. 5, 6. What a family choir these God-given children formed! and they were spoken of by divine inspiration as " cunning " and "instructed." Surely a home so filled with music must have been a place of harmony and love."

Before me, as I write these words, lies the picture of a model and gifted American family, to listen to whose music more than a million people have paid admittance to their entertainments, who are known throughout America, and who enjoy the friendship of some of the most distinguished Americans in the ranks of literature and art.

Including the father and mother they number fourteen. Without one exception, they possess positive merit. For years they have traveled all over America, delighting audiences everywhere with their remarkable talents as musical artists.

They excel Heman of scripture fame, for while he trained up his fourteen sons and three daughters to sing and play under his hand in the house of the Lord, no mention is made of the mother. In this family, however, the mother stands surrounded by her children, a queen, comely and gracious, without whose presence the unity and completeness of the family would be sadly marred.

Few questions are more frequently asked of the parents than, "Are those who appear on the platform really all your children ?"

Until recent years there has always been a baby too young to appear, so the facetious answer was, " No, not *all*, since we have one more at the hotel with the nurse."

The noble mother of this gifted family recently rebuked a mother who said, " I hate the name family ! " with the holier utterance, " I love it, and would always see it written with a capital F."

I append with great pleasure a letter from Mr. and Mrs James B. McGibeny, who as the "Great Musical Family" are so well known, and who deserve so much admiration, and so much attention, as a typical refutation of the fallacy that small families develop greater talent than appears in families where children are more numerous.

New Salem, Mass., Nov. 17th, 1891.

Rev. B. D. Sinclair ;
Dear Sir and Friend :—

In to-night's *Boston Record*, we notice the fact that you have openly attacked " The Crowning Sin of the Age." We hope you will publish your sermon on the "Ethics of Marriage, Infanticide, and Child-murder " and bespeak a dozen copies. During our many years travel extending to almost every city of consequence in the United States and Canada—much comment has been provoked by our large family. Many physicians have talked to us of the "terrible condition " of affairs—lamenting that they were not only asked to do such deeds as made their " blood run cold," but on refusal to lend their aid to nefarious practices were accused of "wanting becoming interest in their patrons," and losing practice thereby.

One eminent physician whose name would carry weight anywhere declared that as a result of this condition of affairs, the medical profession was being filled with " butchers," men who would do anything for money, and that men with intelligence, heart and conscience were being fast driven to the wall by quacks whose main recommendation was their utter lack of moral sense. Many ministers have expressed themselves to us as horrified at the state of affairs, feeling that in many cases they were obliged to administer the sacrament to and treat as brethren and sisters in the Lord, those whose crimes *should* consign them to imprisonment here and to perdition hereafter. And yet they felt the subject " too delicate " to be broached either in public sermon, or private admonition.

So many " confidences " have been thrust upon us, by those who too late, have deplored their own terrible responsibility in crimes that have left them childless, or alienated from each other, that our hearts have been terribly saddened and sore, and we hasten to bid you Godspeed in your courageous attack upon the sin and shame of our land and time. Praying that you may be sustained, we are

Yours very truly,

MR. AND MRS. JAS. B. McGIBENY.

PRINTED POISON.

Notwithstanding the fact that in eighteen states of the American Union there are laws upon the statute books which make criminal and felonious the advertisement of either physicians or other means to accomplish the infernal wishes of unnatural parents, still one can scarcely turn to the advertising columns of a paper, without reading in language carefully worded, but equally well understood, some new and approved method by which parents may destroy the incipient life of their offspring. And this also in many papers which are regarded as respectable, and are freely received into every family, and in some cases papers which bear the name Christian, and are the organs of churches professing the name of Christ!

It is not to be expected that the newspapers, which reflect public sentiment and morals much more than they create them, are to be over-scrupulous in matters which are the current practice of their patrons; but surely the public conscience needs an awakening with respect to the villainous frauds who profane the noble profession which was called into being to save rather than to destroy life!

In the course of the recent trial in the State of New York of a Catskill preacher, for manslaughter in the first degree for having caused the death of his adopted daughter by a criminal operation, a physician named Mackey, when called to the witness stand confessed that he had declared that "if every physician who did this illegal kind of work were arrested, all the churches would have to be turned into jails;" and also that he had answered the coroner's question, "Have you ever done any of it?" "I have" he replied; "but you can't prove it!"

How true is the general charge made by this physician against his profession, we have no accurate means of knowing, but judging from the fact that the number of births in what are called the "higher classes" has been rapidly diminishing in late years, it cannot be questioned that the crime of pre-natal murder is rapidly and terribly increasing. The society of this age is rapidly approaching that of Roman society, of which Juvenal so plainly wrote:

"She who shows no long gold on her neck,
Consults before the Phialae, and the pillars of the dolphins,
Whether she shall marry the blanket-seller, the victualler being left.
Yet these undergo the peril of child-birth and bear all
The fatigues of a nurse, their fortune urging them:
But hardly any lying-in-woman lies in a gilded bed;
So much do the arts, so much the medicines of such a one prevail,
Who causes barrenness, and conduces to kill men in the womb."

My attention has been called to the fact that the great daily in
Boston, *The Globe*, which first printed in its columns the report of
the sermon contained in these pages, reaching hundreds of thousands of readers, sent out in the advertising columns of the same
paper the printed poison which solicits the guilty to practice this
diabolical crime.*

In the classified columns of the Boston Daily Globe of Nov. 9th,
1891, in which my sermon first appeared, are the astounding proposi-
tions of the numerous "physicians" of Boston. In one column are
twenty-one doctor's advertisements, thirteen of them telling the
public in plain English that they can and will furnish medicine
or means to "*women in trouble;*" medicine which "*will never fail;*"
medicine which is "*effective and painless.*"

This is no very great exception to the mass of the press of America. Aside from the startling fact that thus are the rising generation of American women being morally poisoned by the advertising columns of the press of the country, is the more astounding
revelation that physicians are by no means few, and the number is
constantly increasing, who are willing in all classes of society to become the hired assassins of those who would destroy unborn life,
and who often do not scruple to use means which not only ends in
murder, but suicide! Is there no Anthony Comstock in Christian
America who will lead a new crusade among physicians, which will
relegate to the obscurity of prison walls these moral vampires who
trade upon a noble profession, and debase, ruin and kill two of the
holiest attributes of humanity, maternity and paternity?

The home, the great and sacred inheritance of America from the
Teutonic races, the foundation of all that is dear to a virtuous state
and a happy people is surely worthy of all the effort and all the
conflict which loyalty to these high interests demand from men.

THE SERMON A BLESSING.

One of the critics had this to say of the sermon contained in this
book. "The sensational sermon delivered by a preacher of the
gospel in Newburyport, a few weeks ago has attained the object of
extensive circulation. We fail to see how any good can come out

* The paradoxes of criminality would afford an interesting study. A physician
informed me that a woman who heard a sermon upon this subject, went immediately
home from church and performed an abortion on herself, with nearly fatal results,
being only saved from death by the most assiduous attention from the physician!
He further informed me that she remarked that she "would see whether a clergyman should interfere with her liberty in such a matter!"

of such an outburst, and the facts of the case are not such that any man in the preacher's position can know. It is a mistake to believe that a sensational attack upon the public morals effects anything. It repels the honest, is looked upon as a sensation by the indifferent, and does not injure the guilty."

As if by a special interposition of Providence, the following letter from a sweet Christian woman, living in a town in Massachusetts, came to me about the same time this criticism was made.

No verbose rhetoric, or lengthened argument can add one whit to the cogent force of the facts therein contained, as a definite reply to the assumptions of the critic that the sermon has done and can do no good. The facts upon which the sermon is based and against which it is directed, are so patent, and so universal that it requires mental or moral obliquity not to have knowledge of them. Neither is this knowledge confined to the learned professions. The cry comes from almost every hamlet and village in America, and scores of letters have poured in upon me to prove that the vice is not only widespread, but increasingly so, extending to the uttermost geographical as well as social limits.

"Rev. B. D. Sinclair,—

I want to thank you for your sermon of last Sunday, for the good it has done one woman. I have a tiny, little, blue-eyed, pure woman for a friend, who the evening before her marriage was called upon by a *deacon's* wife, to give her a little advice on the marriage relation, somewhat after the manner of women you spoke of in your sermon. She has been most tenderly blessed since marriage with six dear little children. But with each one has come the terribly sarcastic remarks from her husband's family, who try to convince the father that the mother of his children is 'beastly,' 'dragging him down.' The husband had really seemed to be getting ashamed of her until she was nearly heart-broken, but could not consent to comply with his mother's request that she commit abortion.

I took over the paper containing extracts from your sermon, and it showed the husband a few facts in a new light to him, and *the wife is a happy little woman again.*

To me who during seven years of married life has never had a living child, the six little baby faces are glimpses of heaven, and soften many a weary hour when my heart mourning for children seems nearly bursting. I hope that when your life's journey may be ended your entrance into heaven may be heralded by the thousands of little innocents in whose behalf you so fearlessly spoke last Sunday. May God bless you for your heaven sent words, for did not Jesus himself teach us the most tender lessons of *little children?*
Very truly,
A LOVER OF CHILDREN."

The above is by no means an isolated or exceptional case, even of the many instances which, unsolicited or unsought, have come to me through letters, since the publication of my sermon. The sinful interference of hypocritical relatives, in homes which would otherwise be heavens upon earth, cries out for every utterance and influence for its suppression. A case authentically reported to me is as follows. After the clergyman had pronounced a happy couple man and wife, and the new made husband had brought his youthful and innocent bride to his father's home, his mother crushed the trembling heart of the new made wife as she stood upon the threshold of her new home with words worthy of a Lucretia Borgia. The satanic edict was, "Now mind you! there are to be no children in your family." May God direct this sermon to all such hearts with the convicting truth, that such an utterance is a sin against God, a crime against humanity, in short murder!

A SUGGESTION.

From a Roman Catholic physician of Dover, New Hampshire:

My Dear Sir:

Having read your sermon as abstracted in the daily press, I wish to extend to you my sincere congratulations for your fearless exposure of the crime of New England. Regarding your ideas on the sacred state of matrimony, your views and mine are identical. In regard to these evils, the hasty and ill-fitting marriages are one of the prime reasons for the greater crime. Do you not think that the obligatory publishing of the bans would be a check to a certain extent on these marriages? In New Hampshire, a runaway couple can be married in a very few minutes with very little trouble. Only a year or so ago a young couple were married here whose ages were seventeen and fifteen. I am a Roman Catholic, but believe as you do that criminal abortion is fast wiping out the original race, whose place is being filled by the foreigner. I believe there are as many more births each year in this city of foreign parentage, than of native parents. I believe that female extravagance deters many a pure young man from entering into the holy state of matrimony. Hoping I have not trespassed too much on your time I am, reverend sir, very respectfully,

M. B. SULLIVAN.

THE DECAY OF NEW ENGLAND.

The decay of New England, the abandonment of its farms, and the replanting of its territory with alien races, is a matter of current comment. But much that is said is the result of casual observation, rather than careful investigation of authentic statistics and undeniable facts.

To some minds figures have such potency that nothing else will take their place. They desire to know the exact facts.

The demand for statistics is a reasonable one, for only in this way can we reach an intelligent diagnosis of the case, that will enable us accurately to determine what is the real situation that confronts us, and the reason for the alarm which the writer feels, in common with all who are advised as to the real condition of things.

While the writer has been aroused to use great plainness of speech concerning "The Crowning Sin of the Age," more by reason of its blighting presence and nefarious and wicked quality, wherever it has appeared, he is not blind to the fact that "statistics" fully warrant his zeal and his indignation.

Investigation has only deepened his convictions, and magnified the gigantic evil which he has attacked. If the sin condemned is a terrible one in the sight of God, a search into public documents and census reports only discloses the fact that the evil is one of awful magnitude in the eye of the statistician and the patriot.

In the history of nations the birth rate has always been regarded as a question of the utmost importance.

It is an axiom of political economy that the birth rate invariably indicates the rise and fall of national prosperity.

Near the close of the last century, Malthus, after making a careful survey of all of the nations of the earth, selected the United States, —and virtually New England, that being the most populous part,— upon which to base his theory of population.

Observing that the inhabitants of these states, at that time doubled in twenty-five years by natural increase, he considered that fact afforded most favorable indications of prosperity. At that time the birth rate was high, families were larger, and few were found without children. Forty or fifty years ago, large families, numbering six, eight, ten and twelve were quite common. Now they are exceedingly rare. In the great majority of American families in New England only one or two children are found, and in very many families not *one*. I have made a careful abstract from the vital statistics of the Commonwealth of Massachusetts, 1882 to 1890 a period of eight years, which I append.

BIRTHS.

From 1882 to 1890	Both Parents American.	Both Parents Foreign.	Am. Father. For.Mother.	For. Father Am. Mother	Unknown.
Totals.	174,632	193,133	42,801	45,139	8,162

DEATHS.

From 1882 to 1890.	Nativity American.	Nativity Foreign.	Unknown.
Totals.	265,249	86,345	3,432

By adding the 3,432 "unknown" deaths to the number of deaths of foreign nativity, which makes 89,777, we find that the excess of deaths of native born over foreign born is no less than 175,472!

From the above tables, it will be seen that there were born to the native or American born, during the eight years named, 174,632 children, and that the deaths of native Americans during the same period were 265,249. In other words the deaths of native Americans, exceeded the births by 90,617.

On the other hand during the same eight years from 1882 to 1890, to the inhabitants of foreign birth there were born 241,184 children, while the deaths of foreign born, were 86,345; the births exceeding the deaths by 154,839.

In making this computation, the births of children, when one parent was foreign, were added in one grand total, and one-half of that number was added to the totals of both American and native births. It will thus be seen that while according to the Mass.

State census of 1885, the total foreign population of the state was 526,867, or 27.13 per cent. of the total population, the foreign population contributed 18,501 more births than the American parents, or 9,250 1-2 more than half the births occurring in the state, during that period.

Or what is more to the point, the foreign population, consisting of only of a fraction over one-fourth the total population of Massachusetts, gave birth to much over one-half the children born in the state during the eight years from 1882 to 1890.

It has been argued in reply to these startling figures, that the death rate among children of foreign parentage is so greatly in excess of those of American homes, that these statistics do not mean so much as they would seem: that children in Catholic and foreign families die in great numbers, while children of American families are better cared for, and outstrip the more numerous children of foreign born parents in the race of life.

Believing, from a mere superficial observation of the question that these claims were not true, I have found upon investigation that statistics do not bear those out who assert them.

In the report of the Massachusetts Census for 1885,* I find that while the mothers having purely native parentage "have relatively a slightly larger proportion of their children living, than the mothers having purely foreign parentage," yet it is out of all proportion to the great excess of the foreign birth rate. And it is enormously out of proportion to the excess of foreign births over deaths. In the same place it is stated that while the mothers having purely native parentage have 71.14 per cent. of their children living, the mothers having purely foreign parentage have 67.15 per cent. of their children living, or a difference of only 3.99 per cent.

This surely is a very small disparity when we consider the wealth, the culture, the intelligence, and in many cases the luxurious homes of native parents, and on the other hand the trials, necessities, the poverty, the ignorance, and in many cases the struggles of an immigrant population of foreigners. The Chief of the Mass. Bureau of Statistics very wisely and correctly remarks upon this very point, that even with this small disparity " there undoubtedly are limitations and exceptions in special cases."

The *British American Citizen*, of Boston, in its issue of Apr. 5th, 1890, contained the following :—

*Vol. 1, part 2, Analysis p. CXIV.

"A Suggestive Contrast. Last week the health officers inspected a two-story tenement house in the South Cove,* and found four families with six, nine, ten, and eleven children in each, respectively.

"Wanted. A girl for general housework—family consists of father, mother, and daughter of fifteen years. Apply at No.— Commonwealth Avenue."

There are however, certain qualifying facts to be considered, which are thus stated by H. L. Hastings:

"In comparing the birth rate of the native New England stock with the birth rate of that portion of the population which are of foreign birth or blood, it must not be forgotten, that during the last fifty years New England has been drawn upon to people three thousand miles of western territory; and that she has also suffered from the depletion caused by a terrible war; since which she has also sent forth a large Southward emigration. This Westward and Southward emigration has drained New England of the most vigorous, enterprising, and *prolific* portion of her population, who have gone forth to influence society and mold the destinies of other portions of the republic, leaving behind the aged, the enfeebled, and the unmarriageable portion of the population.†

On the contrary, the foreign born element which has entered New England, is to a great extent the more youthful, vigorous, enterprising, marriageable and prolific foreign element, which by its emigration has left Ireland as badly depleted as New England has been by Westward emigration, with a decreasing population and a comparatively low marriage rate and birth rate there. Another qualifying fact should also be noted. The foreign element in New England is now in a far more prosperous condition than ever it was before, and this prosperity is favorable to their increase. They have come out of poverty and squalor into plenty and prosperity, and they have made this change without undergoing those hardships of pioneer life which were braved by the original New England stock, whose descendants are also still doing pioneering in the wild regions of the far West.

Further, the females of the foreign element which has entered New England were not under the domination of the pernicious fashions which have so largely controlled New England women,

*The "South Cove is a section containing foreign population.

†For a further discussion of this subject, consult "*Old England and New England*," by H. L. Hastings.

and which, by the compression of the vital organs, have utterly
unfitted many New England women for the sacred duties of motherhood; but present appearances indicate that unless there is some
caution given or reform instituted, in a few years the descendants
of the foreign population of New England will be quite as fashionable, as stylish, as tightly laced, as slender, as consumptive, as pallid, as short-lived, and as entirely unfit for the duties of motherhood,
as many of the women of the older New England stock have been
for a generation past.

But these facts important as they are, do not invalidate the
general conclusion that New England's decay is the result of New
England's sin in the perversion of the institution of marriage."

The object of this book in the writer's heart has been to hallow
and sanctify the marriage relation and the home. These two ideas
ought to be sacred in every human heart. The "small families" of
New England and America, and the childless mothers of the land,
are occasioned by a profanation or depletion of married life. The
statistics of the Mass. census of 1885 are equally instructive and
enlightening upon this point, as appears from the following table.

COMPARATIVE CONJUGAL CONDITION.

(The figures given are per cent. of whole number of each class.)

	Foreign Males.	Foreign Females.
Single.	37.48 per cent.	36.70 per cent.
Married.	57.31 per cent.	49.45 per cent.

	Native Males.	Native Females.
Single.	63.85 per cent.	59.89 per cent.
Married.	33.17 per cent.	31.85 per cent.

The percentage above enumerated is the per cent, not in proportion to the total number of married or single in the state, but it is the per cent of married or single to the total number of persons in each class. For example, we find that 63.85 per cent of all the native male population of Mass. is unmarried, while only 37.48 per cent of the total foreign male population is unmarried.

And while only 36.70 per cent. of foreign females are single, we find that 59.89 per cent. of the native American female population of the state are unmarried. Or, stated differently : two-thirds of the native females of Massachusetts are unmarried, as against one-third married; while of the foreign born females the percentage of the married is much larger, being 13 per cent. more than foreign single women.

Sometimes we hear it stated,—though the statement is entirely misleading—that the celibacy of native women in Massachusetts is due to the large excess of 76,373 women over the men.

Convincing as such a claim might be at first sight, it loses all its force when we find that while this is partly true, there are at the same time 4,012 more single American males in Massachusetts than single American females.

As a matter of fact, the statement is not true. There are not 76,373 more *women* than men, but 76,373 more *females* than *males* in the Commonwealth of Massachusetts.

The people who say 76,373 more " women," picture to themselves the vast body of marriageable girls, massed in a hollow square and looking about them in vain, from Cape Cod to the Hoosac tunnel, for non-existent husbands !

The fact really is, that these 76,373 females, include infants in arms, lunatics, sisters of charity, unfortunates and ladies of eighty. A large part of the excess is due to the greater longevity of women, and the number comprises the great mass of widows, who have once in their lives possessed husbands of their own, and have outlived them; partly because they are as a rule, younger, partly because of their superior constitutions, and partly because men have perished through war or exposure, or have destroyed themselves through indulgence in vice, stimulants, and narcotics.

Looking at these figures then in their simplest form, the population of Mass., according to the Census of 1885, consisted of 932,884 males and 1,009,257 females. We find that the actual proportion of the sexes is 100 males to 108 females. This makes about eight females in every hundred, including babies, widows, insane and so forth, who have not a complementary male for them.

But this does not much more than cover the relative number of women who are debarred from marriage, or who from prudential, sentimental, or other motives, would not submit to marriage under any circumstances.

And if the marriageable men and women only are reckoned in this calculation, the disproportion sinks to an insignificant fraction.

The statistics are equally surprising, in their general results, when we compare these last figures with the relative number of males and females, married and single, among the foreign born. We thus see that there is an excess of 11,937 foreign single females over foreign single males, and that there was by the census of 1885, five hundred and ninety more married men than married women among the foreign born.

These statistics utterly overturn the theory here controverted. I subjoin the following instructive table.

CONJUGAL CONDITION OF THE POPULATION.

Conj. Condition.	Males.		Females.		Excess of Females.	
Total.	Native.	Foreign.	Native.	Foreign.	Native.	Foreign.
The State.	688,284	244,600	726,990	282,267	38,706	37,667
Single.	439,443	91,665	435,436	103,602	—4,012	11,937
Married.	228,276	140,181	231,538	139,591	3,262	—590
Widowed.	19,573	12,581	58,361	38,797	38,788	26.216
Divorced.	905	132	1,655	264	750	132
Unknown.	82	41	——	13	—82	—28

Perhaps equally astonishing, to some, and bearing with wonderful force on the subject under discussion is the fact that according to the Census of 1885 of the 2,956 divorced people in the State of

Mass. 2,560 are native born, and only 396 are foreign born. How powerfully do these facts support some of the generalizations on public morals, made in the sermon on "The Crowning Sin of the Age," and justify the remark quoted from Joseph Cook:

"Three hundred thousand divorces in this country the last twenty years! Then you say there isn't any need of revivals and outpourings of the Holy Spirit. If our nation rushes on in sin as it is going now I do not wonder that the Adventist says the world is coming to an end shortly. If the brakes are not put on, and there are not general revivals in the cities, and a much deeper work of grace upon the hearts of God's people, and they turn to the Lord, there will be a winding up of all things here."

Full statistics for the United States are not yet attainable ; but all evidence and investigation indicate that these figures are growing more ominous, every year, in every point to which I have referred.

THE UNITED STATES CENSUS BULLETIN NO. 175,

dated April 8th, 1892, strikingly confirms this conclusion. With the single exception of Vermont, there has been a very material increase since 1880 in the number of foreign born in the New England States. The largest percentage of increase is found in New Hampshire, being 56.26 per cent. In Massachusetts there has been an increase in foreign born since 1880 of 213,646, or 48.17 per cent, as against an increase from 1870 to 1880 of 90,172, or 25.52 per cent. In Rhode Island the increase in foreign born since 1880, is 32,312 or 43.67 per cent, as against an increase from 1870 to 1880 of 33.57 per cent.

In Connecticut the increase in foreign born since 1880 numbers 53,516, or 41.17 per cent, while from 1870 to 1880 the increase was only 16,353, or 14.39 per cent. In Maine there has been an increase in foreign born since 1880 of 34.10.

The whole number of foreign born persons in all the New England States in 1890 was 1,142,339, while the whole number of foreign born persons in 1880 was 793,612. There has been an increase in foreign born, during the ten years in New England of 348.727, or 43.94 per cent, as against an increase in native born of 341,480, or 10.62 per cent! The whole number of native born inhabitants in 1890 being 3,558,406 as against 3,216,917 in 1880.

The increase in native born from 1850 to 1890 has been 1,136,539 or 46.93 per cent, while the foreign born have increased during the same period 836,090 or 273.01 per cent!

Prior to 1880 no separate classification of the population, was made by the U. S. Census as to native and foreign born. In 1880, however, the white population was classified as native white and foreign white, while in 1890 a further classification has been made for native white according to Parentage. Under this classification *native parentage* includes all native white persons having both parents native born, or one parent native born, and one parent for whom the birthplace was returned as "unknown;" as well as all cases when for native white persons, the birthplace of both parents was reported as unknown.

Under foreign parentage are included all native white persons having one or both parents foreign born, the fraction less than one-hundred per cent in the first column being the colored population, which are left out of reckoning.

WHITE POPULATION OF NEW ENGLAND ACCORDING
TO PARENTAGE 1890.

Total White	Native Born White			Foreign Born White
	Total	NativeParents	ForeignParents	Total
Per Cent	Per Cent	Per Cent	Per Cent	Per Cent
98.90	74.79	51.82	22.97	24.20
Maine 99.72	87.82	76.65	11.17	11.90
N. H. 99.82	80.64	67.36	13.28	19.18
Vermont 99.70	86.46	67.76	18.70	13.24
Mass. 98.95	69.76	42.67	27.09	29.19
Rhode Island 97.99	67.10	39.81	27.29	30.69
Conn. 98.28	73.74	47.87	25.87	24.54

It will be interesting and surprising thus to note that the foreign white in New England in 1890 represent 24.20 per cent of the total population, while in 1880 they were but 19.73 per cent. In Maine the

foreign white have increased from 9.04 per cent in 1880 to 11.90 per cent in 1890; in New Hampshire from 13.32 per cent to 19.18 per cent; in Vermont from 12.32 per cent to 13.24 per cent; in Massachusetts from 24.79 per cent to 29.19 per cent; in Rhode Island from 26.70 per cent to 30.69 per cent, and in Connecticut from 20.83 per cent to 24.54 per cent.

The Native white of foreign parents, that is, one or both parents foreign born, in 1890 represent in all New England 22.97 per cent of the total population; this element being very nearly equivalent to the foreign white element just considered. The highest percentages reported are 27.29 per cent for Rhode Island, 27.09 per cent for Massachusetts, and 25.87 per cent for Connecticut. In Vermont 18.70 per cent, in New Hampshire 13.28 per cent, and in Maine 11.17 per cent of the total population are native white of foreign parents.

In Massachusetts and Rhode Island hardly two-fifths of the population are of purely native stock, that is, native white of native parentage, the exact percentages being 42.67 for Massachusetts and 39.81 for Rhode Island, while not quite one-half, or 47.87 per cent, of the population of Connecticut are so constituted. Two-thirds of the population of Vermont, and of New Hampshire, or 67.76 and 67.36 per cent, respectively, are purely of native origin, while for Maine fully three-fourths are of native stock, or 76.65 per cent. For New England as a whole, the native white of native parents represent only 51.82 per cent of the total population!

Equally surprising to the uninformed on this vital question, is an investigation of the tables of the U. S. Census for 1890, in reference to a comparison of native and foreign born in each city and town of New England.

In Maine, the highest percentages of foreign born are found in Biddeford, where it has risen in 1890 to 43.55 per cent, as against 35.65 per cent in 1880, and in Lewiston, where the foreign born have increased from 35.05 in 1880 to 39.46 in 1890.

In New Hampshire, the highest percentage of foreign born is found in Manchester, being 45.53 per cent as compared with 38.24 per cent in 1880. In Nashua the percentage of foreign born has increased from 26.61 in 1880 to 32.54 in 1890.

In Massachusetts, of the 47 cities and towns considered, 18 show a larger percentage of foreign born *than is reported for the state as a whole.* The highest percentage is found in Fall River, where more than half the population or 50.72 per cent, are foreign born. This percentage is slightly greater than was returned in 1880, when the percentage of foreign born was 48.15. In Holyoke 47.89 per cent of the population in 1890 were foreign born, this being a slight decrease in the percentage in 1880, or 49.81 per cent. The percentage of foreign born in 1890 in Lawrence was 45.95 as against 44.10 per cent in 1880; in Lowell 44.53 in 1890 as against 38.76 in 1880; in Chicopee 43.60 in 1890 as against 39.93 in 1880; in Clinton 40.37 in 1890 as against 36.74 in 1880. The percentage of foreign born in 1890 is between 30 and 40 per cent of the population in Adams, Boston, Brookline, Cambridge, Fitchburg, Gloucester, New Bedford, Quincy, Woburn, and Worcester. In Boston the percentage of foreign born has risen from 31.64 in 1880 to 35.27 in 1890.

The highest percentages of foreign born in Rhode Island are found in Lincoln, or 48.75 per cent in 1890, as against 47.05 per cent in 1880; in Woonsocket, or 46.49 per cent in 1890, as against 45.67 per cent in 1880; and in Cumberland, or 43.96 per cent in 1890 as against 38.32 per cent in 1880. The percentage of foreign born in 1890 in Pawtucket was 33.87, in Johnston 33.86, and in Warwick 36.45.

In Connecticut, 38.09 per cent of the population of Manchester in 1890 was foreign born as against 31.99 per cent in 1880. Other large percentages in 1890 are 36.30 for Ansonia, 34.83 for New Britain, 35.69 for Vernon, 33.40 for Waterbury, 31.74 for Meriden, and 30.41 for Willimantic. The foreign born of Bridgeport represent 29 per cent of its population, of Hartford 27.16 per cent, and of New Haven 28.27 per cent.

From this brief and general survey it may be safely concluded that it is not a pessimistic prophecy when I affirm that as things are going, the present native population and their descendants will not rule the State of Massachusetts, a single generation hence.

This conclusion is inevitable in the face of the fact that two or three times as many children are born of the same number of foreign born residents as natives. Two facts appear to be established beyond all controversy. First that the birth-rate of the foreign population, is more than twice as large as the strictly American. Second: That in the country districts of New England settled mainly by Americans, the death rate keeps pace with, and in many cases exceeds the birth-rate, so that there is no addition to the population by *natural* increase. This will do much to throw light on the question of the deserted farms of New England. The Board of

Health of New Hampshire, after carefully analyzing the births and deaths in 1880, to draw the line between the foreign and the American, established the fact that the deaths among the Americans exceed the births by 800. That is, New Hampshire lost just 800 of her native population in 1880 by a deficit of births.

THE MOTHERS OF MASSACHUSETTS.

A careful examination of the facts in the Mass. State Census of 1885 exhibits the same relative comparison, when we enquire who the mothers of the children are. This reveals the same disparity which we saw in the birth-rates, and in the conjugal condition of the state's population. I subjoin the following table.

MARRIED WOMEN AND MOTHERS.

Mass. State Census 1885. Totals with percentages of each class to total of all married women of the State.

	Total Married Women.	Mar. Women without Children.	Mar. Women having Children.
Number.	470,206	82,561	387,645
Native Born.	291,554	58,850	232,704
Foreign Born.	178,652	23,711	151,941
PERCENTAGE.	100.00	100.00	100.00
Native Born.	62.01	71.28	60.03
Foreign Born.	37.99	28.72	39.97

Thus it will be seen that while 71.28 per cent of native born women, are childless from whatever cause, only 28.72 per cent of foreign born women, out of a possible one hundred per cent are childless, and that while about 60 per cent of the married women of the native population, have children, forty per cent of the married of a foreign population, which is only one-fourth the size of the other, have children. Or in other words the production of one-fourth of the population (foreign), is to the production of the other (native American) three-fourths as is 2 to 3!

The table of percentages of children living to children not living are instructive, and I give them a place here for the benefit of any who may wish to prosecute these investigations further.

PERCENTAGES OF CHILDREN LIVING.

Nativity of Mothers.	Percentages of	
	Children Living.	Children not Living.
Native born Mothers.	71.50	28.50
Foreign born Mothers.	66.34	33.66
All Mothers.	68.88	31.12

It will be seen by these figures that while 68.88 per cent of the children of all the mothers are living, and 31.12 per cent are not living, a slight difference of 2.62 per cent, more of children born of native mothers are living; and a slight decrease of 2.54 per cent is noticeable of the number of children of foreign born mothers, as compared to the totality of children of all mothers living. To my own mind, the difference in worldly means of bread-winning, wealth, luxury, and intelligence in the homes of the native and foreign born more than accounts for this. In the face of the extravagant claims made that the children of foreign born people die in enormous proportion to children of natives, these figures are increasingly wonderful and corrective!

According to the most authentic reports the birth rate of the New England States is less than that of any large European nation, except France. And the New England birth-rate as collected in the vital statistics, being based upon both the foreign and American classes, it will be seen that when the former is eliminated in the computation, the birth-rate of the native Americans in New England is much lower than that of infidel France even.

It must not be forgotten, and it must be said to the honor of the foreign population, in our midst, that their religious teaching and practice has almost everything to do with the above figures. Whatever may be said to diminish the force of it, it cannot be denied that the foreign born are restrained from violating the laws which govern the physical system and the reproduction of children, by their religious belief. And from a careful inspection of public documents, I find that this is equally true of the foreign Protestant, as of the foreign Catholic families.

SIZE OF FAMILIES.

In the early history of New England, as has been stated, the birth-rates were high, families were large, and few were to be found without children. From the first settlement at Plymouth in 1620, this prosperous condition continued without much change for two hundred years. Startlingly opposite however is the condition of things to-day.

By the Mass. Census of 1885, it is shown that the total number of families in the state of Mass. are 424,415, and that the average size for all of the normal families of the state, excluding boarding-houses hotels, schools, inmates and charitable homes, was 4.45. This indicates an average of 2.45 children to a family. According to the very highest authority, every family must have at least four children to maintain the present population of the world—a fact which should forever set at rest the Malthusian scare-crow! And when we remember that this average is based upon the foreign population included with the natives, who notoriously have large families, the figures are much more impressive. I have not been able to secure statistics of the relative sizes of native and foreign born families, but the difference is so notorious, that the native families must largely be childless, beyond our most pessimistic view. As a matter of fact we find that in 1885 there were 17,141, families so-called, consisting of one person! There were 70,398 families consisting of two persons, which means a family without children. There were 82,760 families of three persons, which means that the parents had only one child, perhaps not any. And this class was the most numerous class of families in the state, with a population of 248,280.

The most numerous population of the state is embraced in families numbering from four to six persons. They number 179,444 families, with a total population of 865,107.

It is significant and perhaps not entirely a coincidence that the number of families in this latter division is but 792 more than the total number of foreign married women in the state of Massachusetts, and but a comparatively smaller number of population than the total of persons of foreign parentage to wit 919,869 !

It is a well known fact that the large families are of the foreign population, and in the absence of exact statistics on this particular point the above is suggestive !

The marriages taking place in the state tell us a corroborating story. I have carefully compiled the record of marriages taking place in the state of Mass. from 1880 to 1890 with the following results, which will be seen in the subjoined table.

MARRIAGES FROM 1880 TO 1890.

(Compiled from annual public documents of Mass.)

Couples.	Both Native Born.	Both Foreign Born.	American Groom.	Foreign Groom.	Unknown.
Totals.	104,862	55,562	21,925	18.678	67

It will be seen that there were 21,925 couples married of which the groom was American, and 18,678 in which the groom was foreign. By adding these two sums together we have as a result 40,-603 couples, where one party was native and the other foreign. Half of this sum should be added to the couples of which both parties were native born, and half to those of which both were foreign born. This gives us as the net result, by adding the 67 "unknown" to the foreign list, 125,164 marriages among the native population, and 75,931 marriages among the foreign. Out of a totality of 201,094 couples married in Mass. for the ten years ending in 1890, 62 per cent were native, and 37 per cent were foreign. Or, while the per cent of foreign population to total population is 27.13, the per cent of marriages of the same class to total marriages of the state is 38 per cent.

This is a fact which speaks volumes as to the estimation of the sanctity of marriage and the home among the foreign population, and a fact which in the cold logic of arithmetic tells with convincing power the reason why child murder, infanticide and feticide is decimating the American stock, and replacing it in the homes, the state, and the church with "the sons of the stranger."

It seems to be the fact that our fair America, notwithstanding her favored position, with such ample resources to feed and clothe her children, with such magnificent institutions of learning and culture to educate and refine them, with such an honored and glorious inheritance of religious faith and life to save their souls, has entered the lists with India and China in the satanic and heathen practice of childlessness, and infanticide and feticide.

The open door of the ages is before us! But upon this crisis in the opportunity of America to civilize and Christianize the world, is it possible that Christian America has gone back to Lycurgus for her laws of the family and the children, and to Plato and Aristotle for her ethics of infanticide?

The parallel seems nearly complete, between the effete and heathen culture of ancient Greece and Rome, and the acme of modern American civilization. Shall the shadow go still further back upon the dial? Shall America become a hissing and a reproach among the nations, while she vies with infidel France and heathen China and India in preventing and destroying the children which is her right, and the bright hope of her future, the preservation of the American civilization which at Plymouth Rock betokened a new era of prosperity not for herself alone, but for the world? God forbid!

In the course of a conversation with Madame Campan, Napoleon Bonaparte remarked: "The old systems of instruction seem to be worth nothing; what is yet wanting that the people should be properly educated?"

"Mothers!" replied Madame Campan.

What does America need to renovate and repeople her homes, and thus reform her church and state, and make her future as morally heroic and pure as her past? I would cry aloud as with the voice of the Archangel and the trump of God—MOTHERS!

THE VOICE OF THE CHURCH.

Some criticism has been expended upon the author for his temerity in attacking a giant evil of the time. Had he confined himself to discussing and rebuking the sins of Pharaoh and Nebuchadnezzar, of the Antediluvians, the Sodomites, the Scribes and Pharisees, or the slaughter of the Innocents by Herod, or even the practices of the Mormons of Utah, little fault would have been found. But it requires courage to assail the sins of to-day, and to set an iron heel upon the head of a serpent that is hissing and coiling around your feet; and more especially to point to the individual sinner, and say, "Thou art the man;" since all sinners are not like David, and do not repent or cry for mercy when rebuked for their transgressions.

But however the crime which I denounce may now be regarded, its sinfulness has long been asserted by the Church of Christ, and by all whose opinions are worthy of regard. Four hundred years before our Saviour was born, Hippocrates of Cos, the famed physician and father of medical science, (B. C. 460–357) imposed upon each medical disciple a solemn oath, which contained this obligation: "I will give no deadly medicine to any one if asked, nor suggest any such counsel, and in like manner I will not give to a woman a pessary *to produce abortion.* With purity and with holiness I will pass my life and practice my art."

The same oath is now administered, to physicians graduated in our own medical schools. Do all of them appreciate the solemnity of their obligation?

In the ancient heathen world infanticide was no crime. The apostle Paul in the first chapter of Romans fitly describes them as "without natural affection, implacable, unmerciful: who knowing the judgment of God, that they which commit such things are worthy of death, not only do the same, but have pleasure in them that do them."

Infanticide found defenders in Plato, (Repub. V. 9), and Aristotle, Polit. IV. vii.: 16), the latter saying that law should forbid the nurturing of the maimed, and that abortion should be resorted to when population was becoming too numerous. In Sparta the law

(71)

directed that the new born child should be carried by the father
to the elders of the community, who, if they found it healthy and
symmetrical sent it back to its parents to be educated—otherwise it
was thrown into a deep cavern at the foot of the mountain Tayge-
tus. Other Grecian republics destroyed the lives of sickly infants.
Anciently infanticide was practiced without fear or shame, and abortion was a familiar theme for poets and satirists. The Jewish nation,
when obedient to the law of Moses, escaped this terrible blood-
guiltiness, and the Church of Christ, from the beginning denounced
such crimes.

The earliest Manual of the Christian church, long lost from view,
and only recently discovered, known as Didache, or " *The Teaching
of the Twelve Apostles,*" which was written, perhaps, as early as A.
D. 120, and certainly not later than A. D. 160, condemns infanticide and
feticide in words which I have selected for a motto upon the title
page: " Thou shalt not slay a child by abortion. nor what is begotten shalt thou destroy."

Hyppolytus, the Bishop of Portus, who was martyred about A. D.
235, in his *Refutation of all Heresies,* B. IX. C. ii; vehemently
denounced Callistus, Bishop of Rome, for tolerating licentious irreg-
ularities, to avoid the consequences of which, women, reputed to be
believers, began to resort to drugs and various criminal devices to
avoid the disgrace which was liable to result from their criminal
behavior.

From the earliest ages preachers, martyrs and saints, not only in
their private capacity but in the great assemblies of the church,
have denounced this atrocious and unnatural crime.

Christianity first attained imperial patronage under Constantine,
and one of the enactments of his reign declared that "The killing
of a child by its father, which the Pompeian Law left unpunished,
is one of the greatest of crimes ;" and with great uniformity the
church, in its public assemblies or through its representative leaders
and officials, has set the seal of condemnation upon this sin.

Nor are such denunciations confined to by-gone ages. The writer
in uttering his words of warning is only obeying the express exhor-
tation of the highest authority of the denomination with which he
is connected, as contained in the deliverance against infanticide,
of " The General Assembly of the Presbyterian Church in the United
States of America" held in New York, May, 1869, which was as
follows :

DELIVERANCE AGAINST INFANTICIDE.

" It is with great pain we are constrained to admit the increasing prevalence in many parts of our country of unscriptural views of the marriage relation, in consequence of which the obligations of that relation are disregarded by many, and separations of husband and wife and divorces for slight and unwarrantable reasons are becoming more frequent every year. Nor can we shut our eyes to the fact that the horrible crime of infanticide, especially in the form of destruction by parents of their own offspring before birth, also prevails to an alarming extent. The evils which these errors and crimes have already brought upon our country, and the worse evils which they threaten in the near future, make it imperative, as we believe, that the whole power of the ministry and Church of Jesus Christ, should be put forth in maintenance of the truth and of virtue in regard to these things. Many causes have operated to produce a corruption of the public morals so deplorable, prominent among which may be méntioned the facility with which divorces may be obtained in some of the states, the constant promulgation of false ideas of marriage and its duties by means of books, lectures, etc., and the distribution through the mails of impure publications. But an influence not less powerful than any of these is the growing devotion to fashion and luxury of this age, and the idea which practically obtains to so great an extent that pleasure, instead of the glory of God and the enjoyment of his favor, is the great object of life.

It is, therefore, the duty of the Church of Christ to oppose in every practicable way these and all other corrupting agencies and tendencies, and *we especially urge upon all ministers of the gospel the duty of giving instruction to the people of their respective charges* as to the Scriptural doctrine concerning the marriage relation.

We warn them against joining in wedlock any who may have been divorced upon other than Scriptural grounds. We also enjoin upon church sessions the exercise of due discipline in the cases of those members who may be guilty of violating the law of Christ in this particular.

This assembly regards the destruction by parents of their own offspring before birth with abhorrence, as a crime against God and against nature ; and as the frequency of such murders can no longer be concealed, we hereby warn those that are guilty of this crime that, except they repent, they cannot inherit eternal life.

We also exhort those who have been called to preach the gospel, and all who love purity and the truth, and who would avert the just judgments of Almighty God from the nation, that they be no longer silent or tolerant of these things, but that they endeavor by all proper means to stay the floods of impurity and cruelty.

We call upon all to remember that marriage is honorable not only in itself, but in its ends, Therefore all who seek to avoid the responsibilities and cares connected with the bringing up of children, not only deprive themselves of one of the greatest blessings of life and fly in the face of God's decrees, but do violence to their own natures, and will be found out in their sins even in this world."

So far from transcending the limits of his obligation, the writer believes that it is the duty of every minister who holds connection with this great ecclesiastical body to unite in this solemn protest and warning to a sinful and adulterous generation.

Nor does this ecclesiastical body stand alone in its testimony. The Roman Catholic Church in the "Pastoral Letter of the Tenth Provincial Council of Baltimore, Anno 1860," sent forth the following utterance concerning this subject.

THE MURDER OF THE INNOCENTS.

" The abiding interest we feel in the preservation of the morals of our country, constrains us to raise our voice against the daily increasing practice of infanticide, especially before birth. The notoriety which this monstrous crime has obtained of late, and the *hecatombs* of infants that are annually sacrificed to Moloch, to gratify an unlawful passion, are a sufficient justification for our alluding to a painful and delicate subject, which should 'not even be named,' among Christians.

We may observe that the crying sin of *infanticide* is most prevalent in those localities where the system of education without religion has been longest established, and been most successfully carried out. This inhuman crime might be compared to the murder of the 'innocents,' except that the criminals, in this case, exceed in enormity the cruelty of Herod.

If it is a sin to take away the life even of an enemy; if the crime of 'shedding innocent blood,' cries to heaven for vengeance; in what language can we characterize the double guilt of those whose souls are stained with the innocent blood of their own unborn, unregenerated offspring?

The murder of an infant before its birth, is, in the sight of God, and of his Church, as great a crime, as could be the killing of a child after birth, with this aggravating circumstance in the former case, that the unborn child dies deprived of the essential grace of baptism.

No mother is allowed under any circumstances, to permit the death of her unborn infant, not even for the sake of preserving her own life, because the end never justifies the means, and we must not do evil that good may come from it.

We confidently believe that you beloved children in Christ, are strangers to this unnatural vice. Our words, therefore, are the language rather of warning than of reproof. Let these sins, dearly beloved, be 'not so much as named amongst you, as it becometh saints * * * for know ye this, that no one who doeth such things, hath any inheritance in the kingdom of Christ and of God. Let no man deceive you with vain words, for because of these things cometh the anger of God upon the children of unbelief. Be ye not therefore partakers with them. * * * Walk ye as children of the light; for the fruit of the light is in all goodness and justice and truth. And have no fellowship with the unfruitful works of darkness, but rather reprove them. * * * See, therefore, how you walk, circumspectly, not as unwise, but as wise, redeeming the time, for the days are evil.'"

A PASTORAL LETTER.

Addressed to the diocese of Western New York, Jan. 30, 1860, by the Right Reverend Bishop Arthur Cleveland Coxe, contains the following:

"I have heretofore warned my flock against the blood-guiltiness of infanticide. If any doubt existed heretofore as to the propriety of my warnings on the subject, they must now disappear before the fact that the world itself is beginning to be terrified by the practical results of the sacrifices to Moloch which defile our land. There are scientific and statistical documents before the people which fully sustain my remonstrances.

Again I warn you that they who do such things cannot inherit eternal life. If there be a special damnation for those 'who shed innocent blood,' what must be the portion of those who have no mercy upon their own flesh?

Dearly beloved, 'save yourselves from this untoward generation!'"

Nor did the learned and Christian Bishop content himself with this bare remonstrance. But with a righteous zeal and pastoral earnestness so characteristic of him, he published a book devoted to this subject, under the title of "Moral Reform," which though now, unhappily, out of print, was a terrible arraignment of this heinous vice, and did much, twenty years ago, to stem the tide of this iniquity.

SMALL FAMILIES.*

BY H. L. HASTINGS.

Those who have witnessed the rapid increase of families of ill-bred, and ill cared for children, have very naturally queried whether such an increase of population was not of doubtful advantage; and have turned with satisfaction to contemplate the neat, well-bred, and well trained children who in smaller families have received more assiduous parental care.

We ought not however, to draw hasty conclusions from isolated instances and extreme cases. There are small families where children are ill-trained, and there are large families which are an honor and blessing to their parents. There are those who claim that under a restricted human culture, a higher type of offspring may be expected. When the children are fewer they may be more vigorous and intellectual, and so the human stock may be improved. There is, however, another view of this subject. It is the work of parents to bring up children, but it is also the work of children to bring up parents; and where there are no children, parents are likely to be greatly neglected, and greatly lacking in very essential elements of character. Nor do the solitary children of well-to-do and wealthy families give evidence of marked mental, moral, or physical superiority over others. A wise observer advised a man in selecting a wife to " choose one out of a bunch," arguing that the self-restraint, self-denial, patience, experience, and mutual helpfulness exercised among the children of a large family, would produce better specimens than can be reasonably expected in homes where there are but one or two children, who are worshiped, indulged, pampered, petted and spoiled, until they become selfish, ill-tempered, and sometimes insane. Nor does it appear that lonely children, in fine houses, are marked by greater health, vigor or longevity than the members of families where the children are like olive branches around the table, and where they are counted as an heritage of the Lord. (77)

It is true that there are cares and burdens incident to the rearing of children; but the toils and labors connected with the culture and upbringing of a family of children, by no means try the human constitution as do the exactions of society, and the unhealthful methods of eating, drinking and dressing which are too prevalent among fashionable people; to say nothing of the darker deeds, which, while they reduce the average number of children, also largely increase the death-rate among the mothers. And the hectic flush on the cheeks of cadaverish and consumptive women, whose smile is like the grin of a skeleton, and whose laughter is "like the crackling of thorns under a pot," are far more likely to be found among the childless followers of fashion and frivolity, than among the happy matrons whose rosy children nestle in their bosoms in infancy, and rise up to call them blessed in their later years of life. Ancient heathenism murdered helpless infants, and rotted down beneath the curse of vice and vileness of every kind. And in preventing the existence of children, and destroying the weak and sickly, it is possible for human beings to put away from themselves rich blessings which God would bestow upon them. Many of the most eminent of men have been in their infancy so feeble that they were hardly thought "worth raising." A man well known for years as a minister in Chicago, who died the honored president of a college, it is said used to remark that he was such an unpromising child that in a heathen land he would at his birth have stood a good chance to have been dropped into the nearest frog pond!

France, where for so long the Word of God has been neglected and disused, is dwindling under the power of its own sins and vices, and her population, instead of increasing like other nations, is actually diminishing through the smallness of her families. Other races and nations dwindle from the same cause. A. W. Murray in his account of *"Forty Years' Work in Polynesia and New Guinea,"* when speaking of a visit to Darnley Island, and of the prevalence of infanticide there, says, "The rule on Darnley Island was not to rear more than three children." Have civilized nations adopted this heathenish rule? If so, they must abide the consequences.

One of the relics preserved in Pilgrim Hall in Plymouth, is the Fuller cradle. The Pilgrim fathers brought the cradle with them, because they believed in the cradle, they had use for it; and though one of their number died upon the passage, yet they mustered with full ranks at Cape Cod, one child being born on the voyage, and another being born while they lay at anchor in the harbor Are their children following their examples? Or are they content to be degenerate sons of noble sires, and to pass into history as a race which has decayed through its vices, and has perished in its own corruption.

We look with sadness and anxiety upon families where there are only one or two children. Sometimes there is a funeral in such a house; and when the little coffin is carried out, there is left behind it a loneliness for which earth has no cure; but where children are more numerous, and are prized and loved as they should be, the broken ranks can be closed up, and there is sympathy and solace in trial, and hope of re-union by and by,

" Where fears of parting chill
Never, no never."

All members of families cannot be great, or prominent, or influential, yet the chances are that in a large family some one or more will be likely to attain eminence. Some of the most noted men the world has known have come out of large families ; nor does there appear to be evidence to show that the children of smaller families develop greater talent then members of families whose children are more numerous. It is stated that Napoleon Bonaparte was one of a family of thirteen children, Benjamin Franklin one of seventeen, John Bright one of eleven children, Charles Dickens one of eight children, Gladstone one of seven children or more, Dr. William Makepeace Thackeray, grandfather of the noted author, was one of sixteen children. Edwin Burnham, one of the most eloquent evangelists of the age, was one of fourteen children, six of the seven brothers being preachers of the Gospel. The children of Lyman Beecher numbered thirteen, nine of them being the children of Roxanna Foote, his first wife. His seven sons all became ministers of the Gospel; two of his daughters were well known writers—one of them being the most noted female writer of her age, Harriet Beecher Stowe, who was the seventh child, Henry Ward Beecher being the eighth. Daniel Webster was one of five children, by the second wife of his father.

Of the eight children of Peter J. Gulick, missionary to the Sandwich Islands, one son died before completing his theological studies, and six sons and one daughter became missionaries in Japan, China, Spain and the Sandwich Islands. T. De Witt Talmage was the fourteenth child in his father's family. Charles H. Spurgeon was the eldest of a family of seventeen children, and his father, John Spurgeon, was the youngest of eight children. John Wesley, the founder of Methodism, was the fifteenth child, his brother Charles, the author of more English poetry than was ever written by any other man, being the nineteenth and youngest child of the gifted Susanna Wesley, whose ashes sleep in Bunhill field in London, and who was herself the twenty-fifth child of Dr. Samuel Annesley, who was twice married, and whose children were described by Dr. Manton as "two dozen, or a quarter of a hundred."

Who can measure the results of such lives as these? Who can estimate the honor which God puts upon any married pair through whom he sends to the world a blessing like that bestowed upon Abraham in the promise, "In thee and in thy seed shall all the nations of the earth be blessed?"

In one of the mountain towns of northern Massachusetts, on a hillside which slopes westward toward the valley of the Connecticut, on the 5th of February, 1837, the wife of a poor working man gave birth to a son, the sixth child in what finally became a family of nine. The half century which has since elapsed has not effaced from the mind of that mother the recollection of the ill-concealed disfavor expressed in the glances of the relatives who called to look upon the little stranger who had crowded his way into a family circle which seemed to them already quite large enough. But as that venerable matron, after four score years of active, useful life, looks out upon the beautiful grounds and commodious buildings of Northfield Seminary and Mount Hermon School, where several hundreds of young men and young women are acquiring an education such as she could never give to her children; and as she receives the grateful homage of those who, year after year cross seas and traverse continents to be present at the great assemblies which gather there; and as she hears of the multitudes of sinners led to repentance, and thousands and millions of people, instructed, impressed, and inspired by words of truth sent forth in many languages to many lands; and realizes that all this work, wrought by the hand of God, has radiated from the cradle of that little infant who received so cold a welcome from her friends and relatives, Grandmother Betsey Moody is confirmed in her original faith that her sixth child, Dwight Lyman Moody, was, after all, worth raising: and those who know her other children and her children's children, are quite of the opinion that the world is none the worse because she was the

mother of nine children instead of two or three, or even less.
These instances, and others that might be cited, indicate that the
theories of some race-culturists may need revision, and that restric-
tion of the family may involve the rejection of blessings which are
liberally given by the bounteous hand of God.

Reasoning from the doctrine of chances alone, we should infer the
special probability that some one member of a large family would
exhibit talent, and attain to eminence and excellence of character.
And if, as is sometimes intimated, there is likely to be " one fool in
a family," the parents who have only one child and who did not
desire that one, are quite as likely to " draw a blank " as any one
else; while in a larger family, if it be properly trained and guided,
there can hardly fail of being some children who will gladden the
hearts, and do honor to the memory of their parents.

Let those who think they best serve their generation by leading
about a little woolly puppy, while a hired nurse attends to one or
two puny, sickly, feeble-bodied children, consider whether their
method is likely to produce better results than are manifest in those
great households out of which come the grand men and excellent
women who shape the destinies of nations by their lofty thoughts
and noble deeds, who bless their parents by the fidelity of their
maturer years, and who make the world brighter and better by their
dwelling in it.

OUR NEIGHBOR'S PITY.

That day our little one lay dead,
   And we were sad and sore at heart,
And all the joy of life seemed fled,
   Our neighbor sought to ease the smart.
Oh! strange sweet power of sympathy!
   That grief should find assuagement thus!
Our sorrow seemed the less to be,
   The more we thought, she pities us!

And then she said, how blessed was she,
   Since God had still denied her prayer,
Nor set a baby on her knee;
   For such a gift meant " such a care!"
Our pain was stilled by sad surprise;
   New feelings in our heart did stir,
We looked into our neighbor's eyes,
   And pitied her—and pitied her.
             —Daniel McIntyre Henderson.

WITHOUT NATURAL AFFECTION.

Natural affections grow in clusters, and cannot safely be dissociated from each other. They do not thrive alone. A bad husband will not be a good father; an unkind mother will not be a tender wife; an evil minded daughter will not be a good sister; nor will a rebellious son be a pattern of brotherly affection. When one of the natural affections of the soul is uprooted, it tears others up with it, and leaves only ruin and desolation behind.

The prevalent selfishness of the age specially manifests itself in a dislike of children, a hatred of offspring, which is as unnatural as it is unrighteous. The first command which God ever gave to mankind when he had created and "blessed them" was, "Be fruitful, and multiply and replenish the earth, and subdue it." Gen. i. 28. And the same blessing and command were given to Noah when he left the ark and stood upon the earth once more. Gen. ix. 1. The history of Enoch, who so pleased God that he escaped the common doom of mortality, is told in a sentence, which relates, not his emotions, his fears, his joys, or his sorrows, but the fact that "*He walked with God* three hundred years, and *begat sons and daughters.*" Gen. v. 22.

But when men are selfish and women are frivolous, this primal law of God and of nature is disregarded. And when by a long course of evil and fashionable and unhealthful living and lacing and dressing, women have ruined their constitutions, distorted their bodies, displaced their vital organs, and thus utterly unfitted themselves for the performance of all the high and noble duties of maternity, then the way is opened for them to perpetrate the darkest and most diabolical crimes, not only against their own offspring, but against their own physical and moral natures. And the stories of heathen cruelties and enormities are cast in the shade by the guilty practices of members of civilized, and polished, yea, and professedly Christian communities, who, in these "last days" have "a form of

(82)

godliness" but deny "the power thereof," and who seem as destitute of "natural affection," as were the heathen eighteen hundred years ago. 2 Tim. iii. 3. Rom. i. 31. For Mr. Froude, in his life of Lord Beconsfield quotes him as saying that "infanticide is practised as extensively and as legally in England as on the banks of the Ganges."

The perversion of one of the greatest instincts of the heart distorts and deranges all the rest, and leads to untold woes. Without true marriage there can be no true family life; and without offspring and family life, marriage is a farce and a sham. When God had made man, "yet had he the residue of the spirit;" the divine vitality was unexhausted; the creative energies were yet abundant; and he could have made a dozen or a hundred companions for man had he so pleased. But "did he not make *one?*" "And wherefore *one*" instead of many? " *That he might seek a Godly seed.* Therefore take heed to your spirit, and let none deal treacherously against the wife of his youth, for the LORD, the God of Israel saith that he *hateth putting away.*" Malachi ii. 15, 16.

The divine purpose in making one woman, as the companion, complement, and covenant wife of the one man, was to "seek a godly seed," a race of men who should fear and serve the Most High. And such a race must not only be begotten and born in the fear of God, and in obedience to his first command, but also trained up "in the nuture and admonition of the Lord," and amid the genial influences of a Christian home. And no such race has ever been reared in the zenanas of heathenism, the harems of Mohammedanism, or anywhere else where God is not acknowledged and obeyed. To accomplish His purpose and perpetuate a righteous seed, God has ordained marriage as an abiding bond, to be assumed with the most solemn consideration, and observed with conscientious fidelity. The "sons of the sorceress, the seed of the adulterer and the whore," "children of transgression, a seed of falsehood "(Isa. lvii. 3, 4), the offspring of unloved and unloving parents, whose hearts are filled with hatred and murder; inherit the same propensities and passions by which their parents were swayed. Hence such children are born with instincts of vileness and violence, with murder in their hearts, and a contempt for the sanctity of human life ingrained in their very being. A mother who is willing to murder an unborn infant, might reasonably expect her offspring who survived her malice to grow up with murder slumbering in their own souls.

It has been stated that the police records of the city of Paris have shown that in a single year more than ten thousand new-born infants have been fished out of the sewers of that Sodomitish city at the grating where they empty into the Seine. Is it any wonder that such mothers, and their children who escape their murderous hands, should give rein to the basest of passions, light the torch of the incendiary among the costliest palaces, and fill the streets of Paris with periodic scenes of blood and flame, and ruin and devastation ?

The love of offspring is a primal instinct of the animate creation ; and the higher the grade of existence the more intense and watchful is the parental instinct. A man or woman who lacks this element has a sadly defective or a grievously perverted nature. Rightly regarded children are bonds of love. In them parents have joint interest and ownership, and they are the pledges and fruits of the deepest and tenderest affections. From such loving families and homes the church is builded and the world is blessed. From such Christian homes come those who shall bear a Saviour's cross and wear the conqueror's crown. The "godly seed" that the Creator seeks, are found here. "Of such is the kingdom of heaven." "Lo, children are an heritage of the Lord, and the fruit of the womb is his reward." " As arrows in the hand of a mighty man, so are the children of the youth." Trained and held in place, they may aid in the accomplishment of the grandest purposes, and become the arrows of the Lord's deliverance for his people ; misdirected and neglected, they may be scattered as " fire-brands, arrows and death," to perpetuate, not only in their own families but in the world at large, all the base and cruel and destructive passions in which they were born and bred. Thus from homes destitute of natural affection, go forth the murderers, the robbers, the incendiaries that curse the world ; while from homes that are filled with love and peace and power divine, come the Johns, the Timothys, the Wesleys, the Spurgeons, the men of God whose lives are blessed and are a blessing to mankind.

Such are the weighty issues that spring from marriage and from home. The cargo is priceless, therefore the ship must be strong. If marriage loses its sacredness the family is wrecked. In every separation of parents children lose a father or a mother,— a loss that cannot be repaired. Hence God himself has laid the keel of this vessel of human hope, and his hand has joined and fastened and bound every portion of its enduring fabric. God joins together man and woman in wedlock by the strongest bands. The deepest sympathies of their hearts; their highest mental instincts; the strongest attractions of their persons, and the most solemn enactments of divine law, unite to strengthen this inviolable bond; while the most solemn penalties, the most terrible physical diseases, and the most fearful judgments of the Lord who is the avenger (1 Thess. iv 6), are imposed to punish the violation of this divine law, and enhance the sanctity of the marriage tie.

This is the divine order, including purity, fidelity, permanent provision for the care of offspring, and the accomplishment of God's purposes of mercy to the race. Man's disorder involves licentious indulgence, exemption from parental responsibilities, youth without care and age without solace; facility of divorce, causeless separations, and the ruin of the individual, the family, the home, and the world.

It is written of the Lord that "He setteth the solitary in families," and the home life is quite essential to the fullest and best development of personal character. And it is of great importance that persons entering upon family relations build a home of their own, however lowly it may be. The reaching after style and show, and longing for city life is one of the curses of the age. God put man upon the soil, and bade him to earn his bread in the sweat of his face; but men look for easier tasks; they rush to the cities; they lose their individuality, sink into mere ciphers, cogs in the wheels of a great and merciless machine, and finally die in garrets and cellars, and are buried in the Potter's field. The *Madras Mail*, describing an interview with General Booth, reports the following weighty words from his lips:—

"Yes, respectability is the curse of nearly every department in the world. Everybody appears to be above the condition of life for which God designed him. Dig your fruit out of your earth, praise God, and live happily with your wife and children! This is most favorable to health and happiness. What do you find everywhere instead of this? There is a rush to the towns everywhere. Go to Australia, or even Africa, and the cry is just the same. Population is aggregating and surging in the cities, and all sorts of miseries are prevalent. I come to India and here it is again. It is all education. Make your people good, and show them how to earn their bread on the land, and then if you have anything left cultivate your intellect and count the stars."

The idea of marriage without a home, or a home without a family, is pernicious and fruitful of misery. A childless life in a hotel or boarding house, relieved of all those cares and labors and sorrows which develop the sympathies and strengthen body and soul, is often followed and filled up by folly, fashion, flirtation, separation, and divorce. When marriages thus contracted for purposes of mere selfish indulgence, have accomplished their end, or have disappointed the expectations formed, what should hinder their dissolution? Why should persons remain united when they have perverted their own natures, and subverted to the basest ends the union which God has ordained for high and holy purposes; when they have rooted out of their hearts the tender sympathies and choice affections which God implanted there to cheer and bless and brighten all life's weary way? Hence they separate; all is easy; no children complicate the case: no house or home is the centre of their dearest affections and tenderest love; the man and woman have only to pack their trunks and one goes to the right and the other to the left, to waste the remnant of their blasted lives, and die neglected, alone and forgotten, leaving none to mourn or care for them, or to perpetuate their memory on the earth; lost, blotted out, exterminated, but yet destined to give an account at the last day before the judgment throne, for misimproved privileges and useless and wasted lives.

It is a mighty privilege to be but a link in the great chain of life which is held at the beginning by the Almighty hand of God, and lengthens itself to the last generation of human existence. It is a mighty privilege to be made the channel of blessing to remote generations, and to have an eminent and useful and grateful progeny, trace back their lineage from age to age with filial affection and reverence.

The one star that beamed brightest in the horizon of the Israelitish woman was the hope that possibly she might be the mother or ancestress of that expected Messiah in whom all the nations of the earth were to be blessed. And there are children to-day whose lives are not only a benediction to the world which they bless, and to the offspring which they rear, but they are also a perpetual joy and honor to the mothers who gave them birth; and while the curse upon the disobedient and the ungodly only extends " to the third and fourth generation," the blessing and the mercy upon the godly, extends to

" thousands of generations of them that keep the commandments of God to do them." To put away all these benefits and blessings, to thwart the purposes of the divine Creator, to disobey the first command of God ever given to man, to quench the spark of life which God has lent to us in the darkness of the grave, and to cut off all hope of blessing and benefit which may come through children and children's children, is to assume a fearful responsibility; and to make this a mere matter of choice, and root out of the human heart those mighty impulses and motives which God has implanted for the welfare, preservation and perpetuation of the human family, is a defiance of the divine will, a rebellion against the order which God has ordained, of which no devout or reverent person should be guilty.

Against this dire perversion of all the sweetest instincts of the human soul, so abhorrent to conscience and to God, the one safeguard is in subjection to the divine command, and in the culture of those natural affections which are the common possession of all the higher orders of the animate creation, which are the heritage of the whole human family, which have their origin and source in the bosom of the heavenly Father " of whom the whole family in heaven and earth is named," and the absence of which indicates that human beings who lack them are grovelling somewhere between the realms of brutishness and devilishness, with a tendency downward to the pit of darkness and despair.

"This know also, that in the last days perilous times shall come for men shall be . . . WITHOUT NATURAL AFFECTION." 2 Tim. iii. 1, 3.

PRACTICAL SUGGESTIONS.

The Psalmist prayed, "Open thou mine eyes, that I may behold wondrous things out of thy law;" and among these "wondrous things' are the wise provisions by which the great Lawgiver of Israel *indirectly* regulated and restrained the exercise of the mightiest instincts which God has implanted in the human constitution, and against the exercise of which direct legislation and prohibition would have proved useless and impracticable. A few paragraphs from a little book entitled " *The Wonderful Law*," may afford the thoughtful matter for consideration, and perhaps lead the reader to that work for fuller details upon this and other points.

"The law of Moses guarded the purity of womanhood with its sternest sanctions. Outrages upon women were punished with death. The seducer of the Jewish maiden must marry her, if her parents would permit the marriage, and if not, must pay heavily for his misdeed; and while wives taken under other circumstances might be divorced, such a marriage was indissoluble. Adultery was punished by the death of both the guilty parties. Prostitution was a capital crime, and no illegitimate child could enter the congregation of the Lord, or be incorporated in the commonwealth of Israel and possess the rights of a free citizen."

One peculiar provision of the Mosaic Law went perhaps as far as was practicable in the regulation of the social relations of the children of Israel. A study of the fifteenth chapter of Leviticus will furnish important suggestions which are as valuable now as then. The word "uncleanness" in the Jewish Law, did not refer exclusively to material *filth*,—as the slightest touch of a dead body rendered the whole person "unclean"—but the word was restrictive and prohibitive. Under this law sensual indulgence made a man a social outcast until he was properly "purified." And by such provisions the purport of which was probably not fully apparent to those

(88)

who obeyed them—did the law of Moses secure ends which all other human legislation has failed to effect ; preserving the purity of the family, the health of the parents, and the vigor of their offspring ; maintaining the balance of the sexes, preventing overpopulation, and quietly and indirectly effecting results which the wisest human lawgivers have been powerless to accomplish; and this in accordance with physiological laws of which the world has been in ignorance for ages, and which have only been discovered in our own generation.*

"In addition to this, the Mosaic law cast about the weaker sex the most absolute protection imaginable. Nothing was left to chance, to will, to caprice, or passion. The stern law of God stood sentinel over the health, purity and welfare of the wife, and preserved the sanctity of the home. Probably for from one-half to two-thirds of her married life, the Israelitish wife was *tāh-mēh*, 'unclean' or forbidden. That word hedged her about on every hand. The slightest contact with her person, her clothing, her bed, or her couch, rendered any man guilty of it 'unclean,' and sent him into seclusion from one to seven days, compelling him to bathe his entire person before he could walk forth as a man among men, and participate in the worship, the festivities, and the privileges pertaining to Jewish citizenship. Exod. xix. 10–15; 1 Saml. xxi. 4, 5; Joel ii. 16; 1 Cor. vii. 5.

"This prohibition was so *timed* that its inevitable tendency was to *lessen the number of births* which would otherwise occur, and at the same time, according to the laws of the human constitution as discovered by modern research, secure 'the survival of the fittest,' the preservation of the most vigorous germs of human existence,

---

*Renouard, in his *History of Medicine*, translated by Dr. Comegys, makes these statements: "The writings of Moses constitute a precious monument in the history of medicine, for they embrace hygienic rules of the highest sagacity. . . . In reading, for instance, those precepts designed to regulate the relation of a man to his wife, one cannot repress a sentiment of admiration for the wisdom and foresight which made such salutary regulations a religious duty. . . . Apart from the religious ceremonies connected with them, might it not be said that they are extracts from a modern work on hygienics?" But what more than this excites the astonishment of physicians, is the tableau that Moses has made of the "White Leprosy, and the regulations he established to prevent its propagation." *The Bible in the Nineteenth Century*, p. 42.

thus tending to produce a people physically superior to other nations who lived without such wholesome restraints.

"Thus the regulation of the social life of the Hebrew was not left to chance, passion, or blind and unreasoning impulse; but the lawlessness of human nature was met, not by the remonstrances of weakness and helplessness, but by the *stern law of God*, which like a flaming sword turned every way to protect the defenseless, and guard the purity and integrity of the home. And as each indulgence of the natural passions was followed by a period of seclusion, the inconvenience of which is manifest, the natural tendency of the law was to cultivate virtue, foster self-control, school the Jewish nation in continence and chastity, and insure the perpetuation of a healthful and virtuous population."

A leading religious journal, *The Christian Advocate*, speaking of *single beds* has said, "If these were more numerous than they are, a great many people would be better off." What a belated sanitary science now recommends, the law of Moses *positively required* three thousand years ago, and thus removed many temptations to sensual indulgence.

"Such a law, imposed on Christendom to-day, would be a priceless boon to thousands who are walking in weariness and wretchedness toward open graves. It would stay the ravages of dire and deadly diseases, would foster affection, hinder quarrels, prevent disgust and divorce, and produce a chaste, vigorous, self-centred race, superior in moral character and stamina to anything which modern usage and custom is likely to develop; preventing those weaknesses and ailments which send men to unscrupulous quacks as sheep to the slaughter; guiding the erring for counsel to the priest, whose lips were to keep knowledge; and laying a foundation for a physical vigor like that of the Jewish race, which more than thirty centuries has failed to deteriorate or destroy. The continence and the ablutions now prescribed by physicians, were then made *obligatory* by divine *law*, which went to the fountain head, demanding that *men* should be holy in body and in spirit, excluding the transgressor and the sensualist from the house and worship of God under pain of death, and making possible a pure, domestic life in the midst of the prevailing apostacy and corruption. These few Mosaic laws were worth more to the Jewish nation than tons of quack medicines, and

.

cart-loads of books written by physicians to instruct people in their duties in these respects. And though infidels may scoff at them, their wives would doubtless hail them as a priceless boon, if they could only understand their import. And we should see fewer faded women and fewer jaded men, if the people of this age were instructed to conform their lives to the healthful interdictions and requirement of the Mosaic law." *

At every fresh launching of humanity on its course, God gives a considerable degree of strength and vigor, and most children, if properly reared and bred, will develop a fair amount of vital energy. And if girls are properly reared, well developed, untrammeled, and unspoiled by godless fashions, and are well married to kind and faithful Christian men, who love their wives as their own bodies, are as careful of their physical needs and conditions as they would be of their horses and cattle under similar circumstances; they meanwhile living simply, dressing plainly and comfortably, allowing their raiment to be flexible and expansive over every flexible portion of the body;—to them under proper conditions, mothhood may be a joy and benediction. And long after the childless butterflies of fashion have faded, died, and been forgotten, such mothers may live in a green old age, to bless the world by their presence, to guide their families in right paths, and to direct their children with wise and timely counsels in the way of life. God has poured wonderful energies into the human form, and has made such special provisions for the reproduction and perpetuation of the race, that if people will simply walk in his commandments and ordinances blameless, most of the difficulties which men and women apprehend will be found to exist only in their imaginations, and all attempts to violate and interfere with the order established by divine providence, will be recognized as most certain to cause evil greater than those which it is desired to remedy.

---

* See *The Wonderful Law*, by H. L. Hastings. ANTI-INFIDEL LIBRARY, No. 13., paper 20 cts. cloth 35 cts. To be obtained of the publishers of this work.

Commendatory Letters.

From Cardinal Gibbons.

Cardinal's Residence, Baltimore, June 4, 1892.

Rev., and Dear Sir:

I beg leave to thank you for the copy of the little work, "The Crowning Sin of the Age," which you were pleased to send me. The Catholic Church has inflexibly set her face against this crime against the family and society, but her voice has not been heeded where yours is heard.

I thank you for your zeal and courage in tearing off the mask and in exhibiting this loathsome monster in all its deformity. May your efforts in the cause of female honor and purity be crowned with success. Your mission is worthy of all praise.

Fraternally yours in Christ,   J. CARD. GIBBONS.

From Rev. A. J. Gordon, D. D., Clarendon St. Baptist Church.

Boston, June 7th, 1892.

My Dear Sir:

I have examined your book: "The Crowning Sin of the Age." I regard its teachings as sound, its warnings as timely, and its lessons as most solemn and worthy of consideration. May its voice be heard by this wicked and adulterous generation.

Yours sincerely,   A. J. GORDON.

From Rev. John H. Vincent D. D., LL.D., Bishop of the Methodist Episcopal Church, and Chancellor of Chautauqua.

Buffalo, N. Y., June 10, 1892.

My Dear Sir and Brother:

I regard your little book as a wise, strong, brave exposition and denunciation of what is, I fear, a growing evil, and I trust that the book may have the widest possible circulation.

Faithfully yours,   JOHN H. VINCENT.

From Joseph Cook, D. D.

Cliff Seat, Ticonderoga, N. Y., June 20, 1892.

Dear Sir:

I thank you for the copy of your discourse on "The Crowning Sin of the Age." It is timely, trenchant, and courageous. The authorities you quote appear to be well sifted. Concerning the huge social iniquity that you unmask, my friends in the medical profession assure me, that discussions like yours are immensely needed, even among church members in our own time.

Yours very respectfully,   JOSEPH COOK.

Commendatory Letters.

From Rev. Theodore L. Cuyler, D. D., LL.D., Brooklyn, N. Y.

Brooklyn, June 11, 1892.

Dear Brother Sinclair :

Hearty thanks for your plain, pungent, and powerful sermon. It is not easy to handle pitch without being defiled, but you have successfully handled a very unclean topic with clean hands and a clear conscience. The discourse ought to be circulated by the tens of thousands, and read too, with twinges of shame and remorse by thousands of Christian (?) husbands and wives who are guilty of this sin against home, and country, and God. In the days of my childhood large families among our American population was the *rule*, now it is the *exception*. The "Puritan" blood is becoming almost extinct in some townships of New England, and the best native stock is fast running out in all parts of our land. No one danger that threatens our future as a Christian Republic is so portentous as this one at which you have discharged so tremendous a " broadside."

God bless you for your courageous fidelity to truth and righteousness.

Yours in Christ Jesus,

THEODORE L. CUYLER.

From Rev. Charles F. Deems, D. D., LL.D., Church of the Strangers, New York, Pres. American Institute Christian Philosophy.

Church of the Strangers, N. Y., June 8, '92.

Rev. and Dear Sir:

I have read " The Crowning Sin of the Age." It is a prodigious blast. It ought to arouse the conscience of the people. It is appalling to think that while Mrs. Stowe was writing " Uncle Tom's Cabin," there were more white children murdered in New England, than colored people of every age, in all the South.

I shall take occasion to commend your pamphlet in the pages of " Christian Thought," and trust it will have a wide circulation, and do a great amount of good.

Very respectfully and fraternally yours,

CHARLES F. DEEMS.

From James McCosh, D. D., LL.D., Litt. D., Ex-President Princeton University.

Princeton, N. J., June 6, 1892.

To Rev. Brevard D. Sinclair.

My Dear Sir :

I am pleased to find that you are showing great courage in opposing in a manly manner, one of the great evils of our day, which has its foundation deep in New England, and is spreading all over the country. I hope you will persevere in your opposition till you raise a public sentiment which will sweep away much of the evil and secure the gratitude of all right thinking people. Yours ever,

JAMES McCOSH.

Commendatory Letters.

From Miss Frances E. Willard, President of the National W. C. T. U.,
Editor in Chief of the UNION SIGNAL, Chicago, Ill.

Chicago, Ill., June 11, 1892.

Rev. Brevard D. Sinclair,
Pastor of the Old South Presbyterian Church,
Newburyport, Mass.

Dear Brother:

With the intention of your book entitled "The Crowning Sin of the Age,"
I have entire sympathy. To my mind there is not a crime more heinous
than the defeat of God's intention in marriage, whether it be done through
the baseness of man or the ignorance, the sin, or the subserviency of woman.
Most of the sermons I have heard or read on the subject, proceed on the
assumption that the woman is the criminal, but you make that plain which is
God's truth that the men are equally to blame. Many a woman has told me
that her husband said he would not support a large family, and upbraided
her for bringing him so many little ones, his utterances on the subject being
of such a nature that a person not informed would suppose he had no more
to do with the catastrophe, as he seemed to consider it, than if there were no
such thing as mutuality in parentage.

The pulpit and press cannot speak too strongly against the evils that
you and I, alike, abominate and deplore. No sane person can think otherwise than this. * * * * When women stand as I expect to see them
stand, invested with all the powers to which I have referred, they will not
marry for a home, they will not marry to secure themselves from the sense-
less prejudice of an ignorant and old-time conservatism, but they will marry
from pure and sincere affection. When they do this they will *desire* children,
and we shall not see the hideous spectacle of a woman who married for a
home, and who, having no real tie of heart between herself and husband,
really detests his presence, and all that it involves.

Whether we admit it or not, this is the case very often in these days, and
has been in all the past. The woman question in the aspects to which I
have referred, means true unions, constant affection, children lovingly
desired and nobly born.

Nothing else, in my solemn opinion will ever bring about the results
in the interests of which you have made your manly, dignified and earnest
discourse. Believe me,

Yours with high regard,

FRANCES E. WILLARD.

From Very Rev. P. F. Dissez, S. S., D. D., Prof. of Moral Theology,
St. Mary's (Roman Catholic) Seminary, Baltimore, Md.

St. Mary's Seminary, Baltimore, June 15, 1892.

Rev. Dear Sir:

I congratulate you for denouncing so strongly "The Crowning Sin of the
Age," the Perversion of Marriage; a sin the more dangerous and insidious
as it hides itself behind the veil of delicacy and decency, which prevents
preachers from branding it, whilst it does not deter its adepts from privately
commending it even to children.

"Oh, the offence is rank. It smells to heaven." Heaven shall punish it,
and reward you for your generous Christian protest.

Respectfully yours in Christ,

P. F. DISSEZ, S. S.

www.ingramcontent.com/pod-product-compliance
Lightning Source LLC
Chambersburg PA
CBHW031439270326
41930CB00007B/783